Who Put the Vinegar in the Salt?

God's Recipe for a Victorious Christian Life

ENDORSEMENTS

If you want to enhance flavor in the kitchen, the first thing you usually reach for is salt. A dash can transform a dish like nothing else. Linda Wood Rondeau's new book, *Who Put The Vinegar in the Salt?* Recipe for a Victorious Christian Life, sets the table for Christian transformation through examining the history, value, and the character of salt. In chapters that include touchstones of faith, such as fellowship, worship, love, redemption, and purpose, Linda provides readers with a way to embrace the life God intended them to know, find the wisdom to navigate earthly roadblocks, and discover light in the darkness. Filled with rich analogies, inspirational stories, insights from both the famous and the unknown, a wealth of Scripture, and comprehensive study guides, Linda has penned the perfect book for individual and group Bible studies.

—**Ace Collins**, bestselling author, In the President's Service series

Want to lead a victorious life? Linda Rondeau's book, *Who Put the Vinegar in the Salt?*, is a well-researched and scripturally based study of how God intends for us to lead a victorious salt life in a vinegar world. An encouraging read in our uncertain times.

—**Sally Jo Pitts**, inspirational fiction author, Hamilton Harbor Legacy series

This is a book you will read with relish, mark up, and read again. Rondeau writes with insight and wisdom, exhorting Christians to be the salt God designed us to be.

—**Carol McClain**, *Borrowed Lives*

I thoroughly enjoyed this solid but easy-to-read book. Part 1 contains good imagery throughout with meaningful content for all levels of spiritual maturity. What I appreciated most was the many poignant statements that caused me to stop and contemplate. Few books do that! Part 2 is reminiscent of Paul's epistles as it shifts from truth principles to application. Real-life illustrations, examples, and applications are presented. Also noteworthy is the abundance of material for further self-study or small group interaction at the end of the chapters.

—**Robert Lloyd Russell**, Christian author

Although Linda Wood Rondeau writes in a down-home friendly fashion, her words hold the punch of truth and wisdom. With her inviting manner, she welcomes you in and deftly shares how we can be more like salt within the world as Jesus urged us. She helps us see the sourness of the world's "vinegar" so that we'll be encouraged and inspired to live within the world glorifying our Lord and Savior. I appreciate everything Rondeau writes. This is no exception.

—**Kathy Miller**, speaker/author, *God's Intriguing Questions: 60 New Testament Devotions Revealing Jesus's Nature*, co-authored with her husband, Larry Miller

Who Put the Vinegar in the Salt? is a gentle book filled with helpful guidelines for being the salt of the earth. Linda Rondeau knows the value of being drawn to God and the purposes he has for his children. A favorite line of mine from her chapters is: "As we grow in our desire to walk more closely with God, we no longer pray simply because that's what a Christian should do. We pray because our day is incomplete without spending time alone with him."

—**Alice J. Wisler**, award-winning author of *Rain Song* and *Still Life in Shadows*

In *Who Put the Vinegar in the Salt*, author Linda Rondeau has given us a practical guide for authentically living as true, "salty" apprentices of Jesus in the face of the subtle temptations of the "vinegary" performance-oriented, consumer Christianity so prevalent in the church today. She challenges us to return to grace-filled dependence on Jesus's Spirit as our source of power, forgiveness and hope in a world that is distracted and overcome by anxiety, suffering and stress.

—Pastor Steve Johnson

Linda Rondeau's study of the juxtaposition of "salt"—believers who, through faith in Christ, have been made new in God's image—and vinegar—the love of the world and what the world offers is both fascinating and convicting. Rondeau points out that as "salt," we're called for a purpose, for fellowship, and to be holy. And that higher standard is made possible only through the work of the Holy Spirit, given to us through Christ. Rondeau combines relatable stories with in-depth, powerful Scripture references to help readers recognize that a victorious Christian life as God's salt is indeed possible and is God's plan for those called by his name.

—Julie Lavender, author of *365 Ways to Love Your Child: Turning Little Moments Into Lasting Memories*, published by Revell.

Who Put the Vinegar In the Salt? is a delicate mixture of relatable personal stories from Linda and biblical truths told with such candor you cannot put the book down. Linda draws the reader in from the first page through the very last sentence, connecting the reader to deep theological truths without feeling as if you just sat through a seminary class. The very visual contrast between the kitchen ingredients of salt and vinegar, compared to the biblical connection of salt being the Christian and vinegar being the love of the world, will inspire, encourage, and spur you to never lose your seasoning and to keep your focus on the Creator. You do not even realize you have just completed an in-depth Bible study. Very well done, Linda.

—**BJ Garrett**, *Unwanted No More, from Exploited to Embraced by God*

Who Put the Vinegar in the Salt?

God's Recipe for a Victorious Christian Life

LINDA WOOD RONDEAU

Author of *I Prayed for Patience: God Gave Me Children*

ELK LAKE PUBLISHING INC
PUBLISHING THE POSITIVE
Plymouth, Massachusetts

Copyright Notice

Who Put the Vinegar in the Salt—Recipe for a Victorious Christian Life

Cover and Interior Design: Derinda Babcock

Editor(s): Susan K. Stewart, Deb Haggerty

PUBLISHED BY: Elk Lake Publishing, Inc., 35 Dogwood Drive, Plymouth, MA 02360, 2020

Library Cataloging Data

Names: Rondeau, Linda Wood (Linda Wood Rondeau)

Who Put the Vinegar in the Salt—Recipe for a Victorious Christian Life / Linda Wood Rondeau

314 p. 23cm × 15cm (9in × 6 in.)

Identifiers: ISBN-13: 978-1-64949-018-6 (paperback) | 978-1-64949-019-3 (trade paperback) | 978-1-64949-020-9 (e-book)

Key Words: Bible Study, Devotional, Inspirational, Christian Living, Spiritual Growth, Group Study, Spiritual Walk

LCCN: 2020952443 Nonfiction

DEDICATION

Many years ago, after a long struggle with feeling I had failed in my walk with Christ, feeling as if I could not do Christianity, I read a book by Fritz Ridenour, *How to Be a Christian Without Being Religious*. Through this book, I learned God does not expect me to **do** Christianity. He has called me to simply **be**. He will do the work. Once this truth was revealed to me, Scripture opened up to me in a way I had never realized before.

Ridenour's book is still popular, currently published by Bethany House.

Who Put the Vinegar in the Salt is dedicated to Christians who are struggling with faith and reality as they seek a deeper relationship with Christ. It is written with the hope they too will understand God's immeasurable love for his salt.

TABLE OF CONTENTS

ACKNOWLEDGMENTS

The creation of a work of this magnitude is not limited to an author's imagination. I am grateful for the many years I have been privileged to serve in the various churches we have attended. These roles of leadership and teaching have taught me to lean on my Lord and Savior for wisdom, knowing the tasks far exceeded my limitations.

My years in human services and social work have provided me with experience and knowledge as to conventional wisdom in healing relationships and emotional baggage that tends to weigh on the heart and mind.

Thank you to my publisher, Elk Lake Publishing, Inc., for allowing me the privilege of publishing works out of the ordinary. Thank you to my editor, Susan K. Stewart, and to my many beta readers who helped me see the mistakes my brain overlooked.

And thank you to my readers for your encouraging words. I treasure them.

Thank you to my family and friends who have encouraged me to continue on this journey of writing, and specifically for this book.

PREFACE

Many books have been written on how Christians should possess some of the properties of salt. This book, however, is concerned more with how Christians have wandered from God's provisions for a salt-based Christian experience and have patterned themselves after the world's wisdom.

This book has been more than five years in development. For the first few years, I read the Bible from Genesis to Revelation several times, carefully studying those references to God's desires for how his salt should live. This book is the final result of those years of study.

I have drawn upon my many years of church leadership and teaching as well as my many years as a human services professional. Often, I have drawn upon my own frailty and the lessons my gracious Lord has taught me during my decades-long walk with him.

This book is a combination of narrative and individual or group study. I pray the reader will be both encouraged and challenged in their daily walk with the Lord.

But thanks be to God, who always leads us as captives in Christ's triumphal procession and uses us to spread the aroma of the knowledge of him everywhere. For we are to God the pleasing aroma of Christ among those who are being saved and those who are perishing. To the one we are an aroma that brings death; to the other, an aroma that brings life. And who is equal to such a task? Unlike so many, we do not peddle the word of God for profit. On the contrary, in Christ we speak before God with sincerity, as those sent from God.
(2 Corinthians 2:14–17)

Part I: Called to Be Salt

You are the salt of the earth; but if the salt loses its
flavor,
how shall it be seasoned?
It is then good for nothing but to be thrown out
and trampled underfoot by men. —Matthew 5:13

Chapter One—Called to Be New

While cooking one day, I accidentally dropped the saltshaker into a bowl of vinegar. The salt within the shaker was ruined, and I had to throw it out. The vinegar also so contaminated the container, I finally gave up and threw it out as well.

Someone told me I could have sterilized the saltshaker to remove the contaminants. Perhaps. But the truth remained the salt within was unusable.

The image of the ruined salt stayed with me for some time as I considered why Jesus calls his followers salt and how precious we are in his sight. I was pricked with the realization of how a minute portion of vinegar had spoiled a good thing.

When Jesus spoke of "salt" in the Sermon on the Mount, he addressed the throngs who followed him—Gentiles as well as Jews—and his intimate circle of disciples.

How strange to be called salt. I can see those along the hillside scratching their heads. "Did we hear Jesus correctly?" "What's salt got to do with anything?" "Who is Jesus calling the salt of the earth?"

Unlike our common table salt of today, salt in New Testament times, though abundant, was a precious commodity. Roman soldiers were paid with salt, from which we derive our word for salary.

Many theologians have likened Christians to table salt and its properties, a seasoning to induce thirst, add flavor, and preserve. There is a problem with only liking this reference to today's version of table salt. Many scholars believe the symbolism is far deeper.

Many Bible scholars believe the Sermon on the Mount was directed at those who recognized Christ as the Messiah and believed he was sent by God. Though some theological aspects of his divinity would yet be revealed, many already understood he'd come to show them the way to an intimate knowledge of God.

His words, preserved for us by New Testament writers, may have been intended to show those who sought after God, both present and future, the key to living victoriously in a sinful world—a world that not only rejected our Lord but would reject us because we are one with him.

WE ARE NEW

When we accept Christ's substitutionary work on the cross, personalize it, confess our helplessness to obtain salvation through our own efforts, we begin to realize our sinful nature. God accepts us, fills us, and begins a work in us. We who were once vinegar are transformed into salt. We are no longer the person we once were, and we are being transformed into what God intended for us to be from the beginning of time.

> Therefore, if anyone is in Christ, the new creation has come: The old has gone, the new is here!
> (2 Corinthians 5:17 ESV).

Our newness is God created. This newness is not something he refashions like an old garment redesigned or handed down. What he creates is entirely different than what we were before.

When we become new in Christ, we become reconciled to God's purpose and plan for our lives. Too often, we envision this plan as action. In truth, God's plan is for us to be one in knowledge and understanding of our right relationship with him—how this newness will develop and define our lives.

Then why do we want to keep being like the person we once were—a person who no longer exists? If we are new, then why do we cling to the old? Perhaps God's intention is for the believer to become the image of Christ—our true identity and calling.

Let's examine the Amplified text for the above verse:

> Therefore if anyone is in Christ [that is, grafted in, joined to Him by faith in Him as Savior], he is a new creature [reborn and renewed by the Holy Spirit]; the old things [the previous moral and spiritual condition] have passed away. Behold, new things have come [because spiritual awakening brings a new life].

BAKERS KNOW

When ingredients are blended and then placed in the oven, the old no longer exists. A new, sweeter, and more desirable product is created. When an object is changed in this way, the properties change. A cupcake cannot say to the baker, make me into what I was before—a summation of eggs, milk, butter, and oil. No. The cupcake cannot return to its batter form. The cupcake must surrender to the call of the baker—to be what the baker intended, to be used for the baker's satisfaction and glory.

The cupcake batter is permanently altered.

The stubborn cupcake can refuse to be used, to sit on a shelf and become stale and unsavory. However, the cupcake cannot return to its previous condition.

> Salt is good, but if it loses its saltiness, how can you make it salty again? (Mark 9:50 ESV)

God has made us salt for his purposes and for our benefit.

CALLED TO BE REFINED

The new us needs to be refined, like turning crude oil into usable petroleum. Refining is hard and takes time. The elements need to be separated so what is undesirable can be removed. The Psalmist rejoiced in this truth, understanding God separated wickedness from righteousness.

> You put away all the wicked of the earth like dross;
> Therefore I love Your testimonies. (Psalm 119:119)

As the resultant sludge rises to the surface, the refiner can then scrape away what is not good. Wickedness and righteousness cannot abide together without damaging the believer's spiritual effectiveness. The undesirable needs to be removed for the product to be of use.

We cannot be refined until we submit to the Holy Spirit's fire.

WHY SALT AND NOT VINEGAR?

You are probably wondering why I'm picking on vinegar. Vinegar has its place. If one were to research the household uses of vinegar, the list would fill this book, and I might just as well stop writing.

The point is vinegar, which for this book's purposes is symbolic for the world, is not evil in and of itself. Much about our world is beneficial. However, God has not called us to be vinegar. Instead, he desires us to be salt.

He has brought us out of the world to be something different, a people set apart, unique and flavorful so others would be drawn to the beauty found only in a right relationship with the Lord. He has changed us, like cupcake batter, like refined ore. We who were once vinegar are now salt.

If we live like the vinegar we once were, how will others see anything different than what they already possess?

Why would anyone want what we have if what we have is the same as what they have?

In the second century, a young man expressed interest in a new religion sweeping the known world. His mentor, Mathetes, wrote a letter to his mentee, describing his observation of the new sect:

> Christians are indistinguishable from other men either by nationality, language or customs. They do not inhabit separate cities of their own, or speak a strange dialect, or follow some outlandish way of life. Their teaching is not based upon reveries inspired by the curiosity of men. Unlike some other people, they champion no purely human doctrine. With regard to dress, food and manner of life in general, they follow the customs of whatever city they happen to be living in, whether it is Greek or foreign. And yet there is something extraordinary about their lives. They live in their own countries as though they were only passing through. They play their full role as citizens, but labor under all the disabilities of aliens. Any country can be their homeland, but for them their homeland, wherever it may be, is a foreign country. Like others, they marry and have children, but they do not expose them. They share their meals, but not their wives. They live in the flesh, but they are not governed by the desires of the flesh. They pass their days upon earth, but they are citizens of heaven. Obedient to the laws, they yet live on a level that transcends the law. Christians love all men, but all men persecute them. Condemned because they are not understood, they are put to death, but raised to life again. They live in poverty, but enrich many; they are totally destitute, but possess an abundance of everything. They suffer dishonor, but that is their glory. They are defamed, but vindicated. A blessing is their answer to abuse.

When I read this, I am deeply convicted. I wonder if anyone would write this about me? I often fail to demonstrate these qualities. Perhaps those are the times I have failed to live by the Spirit.

Sodium gets a bad rap in today's culture, though the substance is found in just about everything. Too much salt in our diet leads to high blood pressure and edema. Sodium is not the salt Jesus referred to.

In biblical times, salt was an emblem of the covenant between God and his people. In the Old Testament, sacrifices were seasoned with salt as part of the ritual and reminder of the Israelites' special status before God. Salt was commonly used as both a preservative and a cleansing agent.

In what is called Jesus's Priestly Prayer, he asks the Lord for the preservation of all who would come after him. Not for a physical continuance but for spiritual completeness to become the vessels God desires.

> "My prayer is not that you take them out of the world, but that you protect them from the evil one. They are not of the world, even as I am not of it."
> (John 17:15–16 NIV)

In Bible times, salt often contained impurities, rendering it useless. Perhaps that is what Jesus meant when he said the contamination would erode the salt's benefit and why he prayed so fervently for those who would come to know him after he was taken up into Heaven.

Since salt was used as part of Old Testament rituals, Jesus's prayer for his future salt is not surprising.

> "Whatever is set aside from the holy offerings the Israelites present to the LORD I give to you and your sons and daughters as your perpetual share. It is an everlasting covenant of salt before the LORD for both you and your offspring." (Numbers 18:19 NIV)

Perhaps Jesus was thinking how these last days, the days after his resurrection and before his return, would impact his new kingdom. He prophesied the world would follow a path similar to the days of Noah during these times.

> For men will be lovers of themselves, lovers of money, boasters, proud, blasphemers, disobedient to parents, unthankful, unholy, unloving, unforgiving, slanderers, without self-control, brutal, despisers of good, traitors, headstrong, haughty, lovers of pleasure rather than lovers of God … " (2 Timothy 3:2–4)

This vinegar—the love of the world and what the world offers—is a world view putting man as the center of the universe and relegating God to lesser importance. This view seems right and good for those who do not know the Lord. However, this view replaces God as the infinite Creator and Sovereign over all that is and was and is to come.

SALT—THE CHRISTIAN DISTINCTION

For Christians, God's precious salt, the opposite is true.

> For in him all things were created: things in heaven and on earth, visible and invisible, whether thrones or powers or rulers or authorities; all things have been created through him and for him. (Col 1:16 NIV)

The mystery in our salvation is how God has allowed us to retain our humanity and our imperfections, making contamination by the world possible. We are still left with the gift of choice. Becoming a Christian does not negate our human frailties. As humans, we are born into the world with these imperfections. Yet, God calls us to a higher standard, only possible through the work of the Holy Spirit given to us through Christ.

While through the Holy Spirit we have the power within us to not sin, reality demonstrates our human frailty sometimes interferes with God's best plan for us. In those instances, we have an advocate, a path to restoration.

If we confess our sins, He is faithful and just to forgive
us our sins and to cleanse us from all unrighteousness.
(1 John 1:9)

I did not have the power to restore the contaminated
salt in my saltshaker. I had to throw it out. However, God is
in the business of restoration. He calls us to return to him
so he can return us to the pure salt he has made possible
for us to be.

LESSON IN AN AIRPORT

While waiting for a flight one day, I sat next to a woman
holding a newborn. For the moment, the child slept soundly.
We talked about what she might expect in the years to come,
the realities parenting would bring.

"I know what you say is true. But this is my son. And no
matter what life throws at us, I'll only be able to see him
as perfect."

This is how God sees his new creation in Christ Jesus—
how he sees his precious salt. When he looks down on us,
he sees only the perfection he intends for us.

THE ONLY "IF" GOD GIVES US

If we cannot earn our salvation, then how can we be
saved? If someone were to say. "I'll give you a million
dollars if you climb Mount Everest," some will refuse. Some
will prepare and dare to make the venture, knowing the
risks, believing the reward worth the dangers.

Our salvation, however, is a reward, which cannot be
a result of human effort.

He doesn't ask us to climb a mountain. The only "if" God
puts upon our eternal reward is to "turn from our wicked
ways and call upon him."

"Say to them: 'As I live', says the Lord GOD, 'I have no pleasure in the death of the wicked, but that the wicked turn from his way and live. Turn, turn from your evil ways! For why should you die, O house of Israel?'" (Ezekiel 33:11)

God initiates the relationship and calls us to him. The entire Bible is a story of how God woos his people. The Israelites' refusal to allow God to heal them and restore them to a right relationship with him created the need for God's harsh intervention. How the Lord must have grieved over his children's choices. He offered so much, yet they refused to repent.

Christ has for all time completed the requirement of a sin sacrifice in order to restore us to a right relationship with God. Our relationship then becomes one from the heart, not a to-do list in order to get something from God.

THE PLAN FROM THE BEGINNING

God desires to recreate us into the image of his Son. This was the whole plan from the foundation of the earth. The first three chapters of Genesis tell us how God created something from chaos. God desires to recreate us, to reshape the chaos caused by original sin.

But God, who is rich in mercy, because of His great love with which He loved us, even when we were dead in trespasses, made us alive together with Christ (by grace you have been saved) ... For by grace you have been saved through faith, and that not of yourselves; it is the gift of God, not of works, lest anyone should boast. For we are His workmanship, created in Christ Jesus for good works, which God prepared beforehand that we should walk in them. (Ephesians 2:4-5, 8-10)

God intended before the foundations of the world for his creation to walk in good works. Our nature, however, wants to recreate ourselves into an image we have deemed is right for us. God's plan originates with grace, through faith—his gift. The result of salvation is we are God's workmanship purposed to do good works—works impossible to fully achieve (though we may try to mirror them) apart from becoming that new creation found only in a restored relationship with God.

CLING TO THE NEW

Why then do we cling to what is old—to the vinegar we once were before we became a Christian? How can anyone see Christ within us, if our minds are set on our view of the world before we were saved?

Instead of turning the other cheek, we take the world's view of sticking up for ourselves. If someone wrongs us, we look to see how we can get even. The mandate doesn't imply weakness. Rather, God intends for salt to take a higher road than the vinegar of the world.

Why?

Because bitterness begets more anger, and anger begets hostility. Aggression begets its own kind in return. Negative emotions endanger not only our mental health but our physical health as well.

The vinegar of the world would make us believe we are due a full and complete explanation for our circumstances. "We deserve to know," we tell ourselves. Salt leans upon what we know of God and trusts in our restored relationship with him.

The cross is the only evidence we need to prove God's intent for our good. In the hymn of old, "My Faith Has Found A Resting Place," the lyrics remind us of this truth: "It is enough that Jesus died, and that he died for me."

> You have heard that it was said, "Eye for eye, and tooth for tooth." But I tell you, do not resist an evil person. If anyone slaps you on the right cheek, turn to them the

other cheek also. And if anyone wants to sue you and take your shirt, hand over your coat as well. If anyone forces you to go one mile, go with them two miles. Give to the one who asks you, and do not turn away from the one who wants to borrow from you. (Matthew 5:38–42 NIV)

Unfortunately, the world's values have crept into the believer's psyche, preventing us from fully enjoying our relationship with God. Once we have been restored to a right relationship with our father, far deeper even than with a human parent, then we can begin to know the fullness of his grace.

For this reason I bow my knees to the Father of our Lord Jesus Christ, from whom the whole family in heaven and earth is named, that He would grant you, according to the riches of His glory, to be strengthened with might through His Spirit in the inner man, that Christ may dwell in your hearts through faith; that you, being rooted and grounded in love, may be able to comprehend with all the saints what is the width and length and depth and height— to know the love of Christ which passes knowledge; that you may be filled with all the fullness of God. (Ephesians 3:14–19)

We tend to forget God's best is often in opposition to what the world views as our best, because the world measures our value by different standards. Our spiritual richness is only achieved when what we seek from God aligns with what he knows is best for our eternal rewards, not our earthly gain.

Does he care when we hurt? Does he care when our bank accounts are empty? Does he care when men have falsely accused us of wrongdoing? Does he care if we lose our jobs over something for which we had no control, or because we stood up for what was morally correct? Does he care when someone we love is ill or dies?

Of course, he does. He weeps along with us. He is our Father.

Trust is knowing we are saved for a better life. Perhaps God's grace is best shown in the how we approach these matters than the why of the matters.

> Praise be to the God and Father of our Lord Jesus Christ, who has blessed us in the heavenly realms with every spiritual blessing in Christ. For he chose us in him before the creation of the world to be holy and blameless in his sight. In love he predestined us for adoption to sonship through Jesus Christ, in accordance with his pleasure and will—to the praise of his glorious grace, which he has freely given us in the One he loves. In him we have redemption through his blood, the forgiveness of sins, in accordance with the riches of God's grace that he lavished on us with wisdom and understanding, (Ephesians 1:3–8a NIV)

This sounds to me like a God who is invested in his children. He does not pat us on the head and say, "Go on, now and try to be good." He says, "Go now and leave your life of sin" (John 8:11 paraphrased)

We have no right to be proud of our good deeds because any good work is the natural outcome of our salvation, second-nature behavior for which we do not pre-analyze— just as we breathe to live without thinking. We expel air and take it in without analyzing when and how. Likewise, our deeds are expelled from the breath of Christ in our lives.

> He saved us, not because of any works of righteousness that we had done, but because of His own pity and mercy, by [the] cleansing [bath] of the new birth (regeneration) and renewing of the Holy Spirit. (Titus 3:5 AMPC)

There will be a day when the elements will melt and when the world as we know it will pass away. In view of this truth, the New Testament writers ask this question, "How should we live ... how should we conduct ourselves?" In godliness, choosing eternity over the temporal, the spiritual over the material, and the permanent over the passing fancies of the world. Choose salt, gifted to us by Christ's redemptive work, over the vinegar of the world.

> Therefore, since all these things will be dissolved, what manner of persons ought you to be in holy conduct and godliness. (2 Peter 3:11)

FOR FURTHER STUDY OR GROUP DISCUSSION

(Note: Some of the references for the study portions have been provided for convenience. However, whether in group or independent study, you may wish to consult various versions.)

1. Read Jude 1.
   - What three designations describe the believer?

2. Read Isaiah 61:1–3.

   > The Spirit of the Lord GOD is upon me,
   > Because the LORD has anointed *and* commissioned me
   > To bring good news to the humble and afflicted;
   > He has sent me to bind up [the wounds of] the brokenhearted,
   > To proclaim release [from confinement and condemnation] to the [physical and spiritual] captives

And freedom to prisoners,
To proclaim the favorable year of the LORD,
And the day of vengeance *and* retribution of our
God,
To comfort all who mourn,
To grant to those who mourn in Zion *the following*:
To give them a turban instead of dust [on their
heads, a sign of mourning],
The oil of joy instead of mourning,
The garment [expressive] of praise instead of a
disheartened spirit.
So they will be called the trees of righteousness
[strong and magnificent, distinguished for
integrity, justice, and right standing with God],
The planting of the LORD, that He may be glorified.
(AMP)

- To what are we called, sanctified, and preserved?

3. Read Colossians 4:5–6.

   Walk in wisdom toward those *who are* outside,
   redeeming the time. *Let* your speech always *be* with
   grace, seasoned with salt, that you may know how
   you ought to answer each one.

Salt often creates a thirst for more salt. When Christians
sprinkle the right amount of salted conversation, others
will become thirsty.

- How does this set us apart from the world's
  standard?

4. Read Ephesians 1:3–4.

> Blessed be the God and Father of our Lord Jesus Christ, who has blessed us with every spiritual blessing in the heavenly places in Christ, just as He chose us in Him before the foundation of the world, that we should be holy and without blame before Him in love.

- How does this set us apart from the world's standard?

5. Read 2 Timothy 3:1–3.

> But know this, that in the last days perilous times will come. For men will be lovers of themselves, lovers of money, boosters, proud, blasphemers, disobedient to parents, unthankful, unholy, unloving, unforgiving, slanders, without self-control, brutal, despisers of good.

The last days referenced here are those between the apostolic period and Christ's return. Here Paul lists those attributes the world admires.

- What are they?

- Why do you think the world values these things?

- What are the opposites of these values?

- How does this hold us to a higher standard?

6. Read Titus 1:15–16.

To the pure all things are pure, but to those who are corrupted and do not believe, nothing is pure. They claim to know God but by their actions they deny him. They are detestable, disobedient, and unfit for doing anything good. (NIV)

- According to this verse, what is the difference between pure and impure?

- What prompts our actions?

From the following verses, what benefit does God provide the believer towards the goal of living like salt?
- Romans 6:14 _____
  _____
- 2 Cor 12:9_____
  _____
- Phil 4:13 _____
  _____
- James 4:7 _____
  _____
- 1 Corinthians 10:13 _____
  _____
- 1 John 1:9 _____
  _____
- Psalm 50:15_____
  _____

- Our reconciliation means we are restored to a right relationship or standard or to make peace where formerly there was enmity.

7. Compare Colossians 1:21–22 to Hebrews 2:14–15.

   And you, who once were alienated and enemies in your mind by wicked works, yet now He has reconciled in the body of His flesh through death, to present you holy, and blameless, and above reproach in His sight (Colossians 1:21–22)

   Inasmuch then as the children have partaken of flesh and blood, He Himself likewise shared in the same, that through death He might destroy him who had the power of death, that is, the devil, and release those who through fear of death were all their lifetime subject to bondage. (Hebrews 2:14–15)

   - How do we become reconnected to God?

8. Read Ephesians 1:11–12.

   In Him also we have obtained an inheritance, being predestined according to the purpose of Him who works all things according to the counsel of His will, that we who first trusted in Christ should be to the praise of His glory.

   - Why are we saved?

9. Read Ephesians 4:1–3.

   I, therefore, the prisoner of the Lord, beseech you to walk worthy of the calling with which you were called, with all lowliness and gentleness, with longsuffering, bearing with one another in love, endeavoring to keep the unity of the Spirit in the bond of peace.

- Paul acknowledges we have this hope and the power of the living God who dwells within us. What characteristics does he mention that exemplify a life that is "worthy of the calling?"

Chapter Two—Called to Be Transformed

Our world culture is in love with self. Songs encourage us to love ourselves for this is the greatest love of all. Self-preservation is a natural, biological instinct. We innately seek, not only our survival, but our comfort. We seek shelter from the wind, we like a roof over our head when it rains, we look for shade on a hot day, and we want a warm blanket when the temperatures fall.

The Bible also recognizes this human instinct for self-regard. The commandment is not to disavow ourselves, rather to love the Lord our God with all our hearts and to love our neighbors as ourselves.

THE PURSUIT OF SELF

In the beginning, man was in complete union with God and gave no thought to his own body or needs until Adam sinned. God asked him, "Who told you that you were naked?"

Thus, the birth of guilt and awareness of sin.

This human desire to satisfy self can create intense emotions when things do not go as we hope. Perceived need causes us to bemoan our lack—especially when compared to what others possess or achieve, and to nurse our anxieties and disappointments. The wisdom of the world plays out in all we read, our television viewing, and our hero-worship. Years ago, a hit song by Frank Sinatra was heralded as the wisdom for the ages as he proclaimed, "I did it my way."

Psychologists have fashioned several diagrams of self-actualization, the desire to be all that we can be. At the bottom of the pyramid are the primal needs: food, air, shelter, clothing, and reproduction. Once these are met, humans will look to safety and security—employment, property, health, and resources. Next, human nature will strive for a sense of love and community—acceptance into a social group—friendship and a sense of belonging. These things, so they theorize, once achieved, will give one a sense of status, recognition, strength—those self-perceptions that are the basis of self-actualization.

The world might view the process of self-actualization through pursuits—hard work that brings about a desired outcome. In the movie, *Back to the Future*, Marty McFly tells his younger father, "You know, George, if you put your mind to it, you can accomplish anything." This is the world's view of hard work—if you try hard enough, nothing is impossible. If you can dream it, you can do it.

GOD'S HIERARCHICAL DESIGN

God's method for self-actualization is quite different. He is the supplier, our protector, our defender, and our reason for being. When we enter into a relationship with him, becoming the salt he wants us to be is dependent upon our continuing connection with the Lord through the work of the Holy Spirit.

> I am the vine, you are the branches. He who abides in Me, and I in him, bears much fruit; for without Me you can do nothing. (John 15:5)

The quest for self-actualization begins when we are born. The natural self believes we are deserving of basic needs. We believe we are entitled to comfort, purpose, health, or wealth. We yearn to be loved and accepted. We perceive if God truly loves us, then, as the benefactor of our welfare, we should be given what we desire. Especially, if we strive toward a moral and upright life.

Such was Job's thought as well as that of his so-called friends. When calamity struck, they were convinced Job must have sinned, and God must be punishing him. The book of Job brings many to wonder why Job suffered so much, enduring physical suffering in addition to horrendous personal loss. How could a loving Father allow so much tragedy into the life of one whose righteousness pleased God? Our minds are befuddled by our human sense of what is fair and just. Especially when such unfairness is aimed at our own personal welfare and seemingly allowed by God.

In the final chapters of the book, God answers Job, in essence saying, "Before you take it on yourself to criticize my ways, you should ask yourself if you could manage the creation as well as I did." Through taking Job on a journey of the natural world, Job realizes his insignificance, his powerlessness, his ignorance about God and his ways, and Job's finite state compared to an everlasting God.

The reality is we are unworthy to receive anything from God. But because we are born with a sense of self-importance, this reality can put us at enmity with our Creator.

In actuality, our true self-worth begins with the recognition we are undeserving and helpless. Yet, God values us above all. When we stand in awe of the beauty, power, and complexity of creation, we wonder why God bothers with insignificant humankind. We understand why the Psalmist wrote:

> LORD, what is man, that You take knowledge of him?
> Or the son of man, that You are mindful of him?
> (Psalm 144:3)

God esteems us because of his everlasting love for his creation—the reason he calls us to be salt and to live according to his standards, not the world's.

Therefore, as the elect of God, holy and beloved, put on tender mercies, kindness, humility, meekness, longsuffering; bearing with one another, and forgiving one another, if anyone has a complaint against another; even as Christ forgave you, so you also *must do*. (Colossians 3:12–13)

God's hierarchical plan of self-actualization for his people is to bring them into a relationship with him, to repair our state of alienation through transformation. Satan, as he did with Adam and Eve, will throw out a complete arsenal to prevent us from experiencing the fullness of God.

TRANSFORMED TO WORSHIP

God transforms his salt in order to truly worship him in Spirit and in Truth.

"But the hour is coming, and now is, when the true worshipers will worship the Father in spirit and truth; for the Father is seeking such to worship Him." (John 4:23)

To this end, to truly worship, he must reshape us, to bring our self-image in alignment with his attributes. We cannot truly worship the Lord in our natural state—the state concerned only about our earthly life. The Lord must transform us through a new way of thinking:

I beseech you therefore, brethren, by the mercies of God, that you present your bodies a living sacrifice, holy, acceptable to God, which is your reasonable service. And do not be conformed to this world, but be transformed by the renewing of your mind, that you may prove what is that good and acceptable and perfect will of God. (Romans 12:1–2)

Transformation begins with restoration. And, in view of his mercy and great love for us, restoration requires a complete and willful surrender to God's sovereignty. Then real worship begins—not in mindless action but with a heart full of gratitude. This is what Satan fears the most. For when we worship, we are becoming transformed. We are not what we once were, nor are we yet what we will become.

Perhaps the devil's most effective form of vinegar, his tool to corrupt the salt God intends for us to be, is to interfere in our ability to worship.

One way Satan impedes this holy experience is through fatigue.

James Dobson states that fatigue is currently the biggest obstacle facing the family. "It is over-commitment; time pressure. If Satan can't make you sin, he'll make you busy, and that's just about the same thing."

Fatigue can disrupt our physical world. Loss of appetite, inability to sleep, inability to enjoy sex, confusion, and impaired decision-making. All these are manifestations of fatigue. Prolonged fatigue will cause significant physical and mental health problems. We cry out, "Stop the world, I want to get off."

Likewise, our religious practice is susceptible to overload and Satan's harangues. We tire of constant vigilance. When we reach a point of religious fatigue, reading the Bible or going to church, even praying, seems beyond our endurance or may seem pointless. From our human efforts, God seems far away. Religious fatigue, like physical fatigue, drains us of energy.

Is it any wonder the God of love desires his salt to worship him? The question must be asked—did God institute worship as a drudgery or for the benefit of his creation? Not only for his spiritual life but for his physical health as well?

> Seven times a day I praise You, because of Your righteous judgments. (Psalm 119:164)

The Psalmist is not saying there is a required number of hours or times we must get down on our knees and raise our hands to the heavens. What he implies is an attitude of worship—a natural response when we realize our status before Sovereign God. A humility coming from the notion of a perfect, holy, eternal God who has shown such favor toward an insignificant creature such as frail humanity.

Modern psychology knows full well the value inherent by balancing work and play. We also know the importance of social interactions. Yet we relegate the act of worship into tasks rather than simply being. We busy ourselves in our charitable deeds, rather than bask in the presence of God and wonder why we feel spiritually spent.

In the Sermon of the Mount (Matthew 5, 6, 7), the place where Jesus told his followers they were salt, our Lord addressed these very issues. He warned against pursuing good deeds for wrong reasons, public displays of piety, accumulation of possessions, and a preoccupation with necessities such as food, clothing, and drink. "For everyone seeks these things," he says. (paraphrased) He reminds us how God knows our needs. If he cares so much for plants and animals, how much more will he provide for us, his precious salt? God would rather we communicate with him than ignore his presence while preaching about him to the world.

When we seek God first, Jesus said work, play, and love flow naturally from God's miraculous provision. Then we can rise upon eagles' wings and find the purest joy in a child's smile, praising God for the abundance of life around us.

TRANSFORMED TO BE CLEAN

Fatigue is only one impediment to our ability to sense God's love for us.

Unconfessed sin is another destructive element in the believer's life. If we believe Satan's lies, we are tempted to make excuses for our wrongs. We might look at someone else's sin and believe ours is not serious at all in comparison.

We tend to view sin on a bell curve. Some so much worse than others. Why should I feel bad about a little fib when Jack is cheating on his wife? Or we might convince ourselves the much good we've accomplished outweighs our fewer mistakes. "After all, in the large scheme of things," we reason, "I haven't done so badly."

Many church leaders point to Psalm 51 as the model for penitent confession. The first step is to recognize God's mercy ... to remember he loves us. Belief in this truth gives us the courage to confess our sins, to understand how sin— our sin—separates us from God.

TRANSFORMED TO MINISTER

God wants his people to share their knowledge of his goodness.

As an author, I belong to several social media sites. I am constantly amazed at the types of sharing I see. One constancy is the joyful posts when one experiences a surprise, a family gathering, a new recipe, or even a new hairdo. These posts seem to generate the most responses. We love to demonstrate how an occasion or a new dress has lifted us out of the doldrums. Folks also tend to share their sorrows, not leaving anything out. Some even post pictures of the broken bones or surgical encounters.

If the vinegar of the world shares so freely, seeks and looks for a sense of community, how much more does God expect his salt to love one another, to reflect his great love for us? How much more does God desire we share the many blessings he has given us, how he has upheld us in times of trouble?

In Acts 11, we read how Christ's followers were scattered because of persecution. Yet, wherever they went, they preached about Jesus. They shared, even in their difficulties, how Christ came, died, and rose again—offering this new life to anyone who would accept him. Why? Because even in these trials, their joy was immense.

I have several friends who are suffering from severe or terminal illnesses. I am humbled and amazed how quickly and fervently they praise God even when facing possible death. I remember the testimony of an elderly pastoral couple, mentors to my husband and me for many years. Within the space of two days, they unexpectedly lost two sons. I cannot imagine that kind of pain. Yet not a day would pass without this couple giving praise to God for his goodness. The world cannot understand this kind of joy.

Though I'm generally optimistic, I don't know if I could muster this kind of faith if I were in those circumstances. A faith like theirs comes only from a Holy Spirit connection to our Father, the power God gives to his salt—peace beyond comprehension. He wants us to let others know, he'll do the same for them.

We minister through service to others ... not just with our words. We want to serve the Lord because of all he has done for us. Our service is not to get something from God, rather to express our joy by doing good, to serve and to witness.

TRANSFORMED TO BE GOD'S CHILD

We must no longer live like the slaves we once were.

Christ has provided a means for our redemption. When we accept his substitution for our sins, in God's eyes we are now righteous. He sends his Holy Spirit to teach us how to act as perfectly as God sees us ... as his child.

God holds us in his loving arms, cradling us with even more joy than a new parent, and imprints us in his hand.

> Who shall separate us from the love of Christ? Shall trouble of hardship or persecution or famine or nakedness or danger or sword? ... For I am convinced that neither death nor life, neither angels nor demons,

neither the present nor the future, nor any powers, neither height nor depth, nor anything else in all creation, will be able to separate us from the love of God that is in Christ Jesus our Lord. (Romans 8:35,38–39 NIV)

Why then do we live as if we are still orphans? Why do we doubt God's intention toward us?

Perhaps because we turn our eyes away from God and forget he holds us dear and precious. Circumstances may have blinded us to this truth, or we think God has not dealt with us according to what we perceive is our due. We choose to think of ourselves as slaves, rather than a royal prince or princess. We forget Christ has set us free.

We are like that kidnapped person who is chained to a pole. The police have come and rescued him, taken off his chains. Yet, he stays huddled to the place of his imprisonment.

Old Testament law required masters to free a slave after his seventh year of servitude (Exodus 21:5). If the slave did not desire to be freed, his ear was pierced, and he became indentured to his master forever.

Those who continue to live as we were before Christ freed us are like a slave who chooses to remain in bondage when his master offers him complete freedom. We choose to remain as vinegar instead of living like his precious child.

As even earthly parents do, God desires for his children to prosper.

The Lord repeatedly admonished Israel to be a city of salt, like it's holy capital, Jerusalem, to be his shining light on a hill. That the city survives, let alone flourishes is miraculous. When established, the city had no strategic value—no waterways, mineral deposits, or other natural resources. By all logic, the city should have remained an insignificant village and vanished into oblivion as did so many other ancient cultures.

Our loving Father stands ready to make our lives as miraculous as Jerusalem's endurance.

> Know that the Lord is God. It is he who made us and we are his; we are his people the sheep of his pasture. (Psalm 100:3 NIV)

We humans are especially attached to things we have created with our own hands. Think about your most treasured possessions? We take special care to preserve them. How much more does God desire to preserve us, those he called to be set apart, special, unique, chiseled to resemble him, his precious children?

> And those he predestined, he also called; those he called, he also justified; those he justified, he also glorified. (Romans 8:30 NIV)

He made us to be like him. Only through our relationship with him can our true identify be known ... salt ... purified and precious.

This is the work of the cross. Not past tense, because Christ's work is living still.

I especially like the Amplified Version of John 3:16–17:

> For God so [greatly] loved and dearly prized the world, that He [even] gave His [One and] only begotten Son, so that whoever believes and trusts in Him [as Savior] shall not perish, but have eternal life. For God did not send the Son into the world to judge and condemn the world [that is, to initiate the final judgment of the world], but that the world might be saved through Him.

Oh, if we could grasp how much God loves us, how much he invests in us, how much he desires only good in our lives, to shape us into his image. How sad that we refuse the freedom, grace, destiny, and sonship he has planned for us.

> I have been crucified with Christ; it is no longer I who live, but Christ lives in me; and the *life* which I now live in the flesh I live by faith in the Son of God, who loved me and gave Himself for me. (Galatians 2:20)

By living like an orphan, we can become ensnared in our old lifestyles. However, continuation in sin is not God's intention for the believer. We can also become enslaved by popular isms, also true in Paul's circles. No wonder Paul admonishes believers not to be persuaded by any dogma that diminishes the work of Christ on the cross or persuades us against our true worth to God.

> Beware lest anyone cheat you through philosophy and empty deceit, according to the tradition of men, according to the basic principles of the world, and not according to Christ. (Colossians 2:8)

God transforms us to be like him. The world wants to transform us to be like them. The choice is ours.

FOR FURTHER STUDY OR GROUP DISCUSSIONS

1. Read Deuteronomy 10:12.

   > And now, Israel, what does the LORD your God require of you, but to fear the LORD your God, to walk in all His ways and to love Him, to serve the LORD your God with all your heart and with all your soul.

   - In what way is this worshiping the Lord?

   - Does fear (respect/knowledge/love) of the Lord come before "walking in all his ways?"

- Can we truly walk in his ways without first knowing him?

2. Let's look at the Amplified version of 1 John 3:1

   See what an incredible quality of love the Father has shown to us, that we would [be permitted to] be named and called and counted the children of God! And so we are! (AMP)

Examine this verse from different versions. The KJV uses the word "bestowed."

- What other words do you find?

- I like the Amplified translation because it emphasizes that God's love is incredible, beyond definition or comprehension, especially that he would call us his child. How does this impact your desire to worship?

3. Read Psalm 95.

- In what ways to we worship?

- Why do we worship?

4. Read 2 Peter 1: 2–8.

Grace and peace be multiplied to you in the knowledge
of God and of Jesus our Lord, as His divine power
has given to us all things that pertain to life and
godliness, through the knowledge of Him who called
us by glory and virtue, by which have been given to
us exceedingly great and precious promises, that
through these you may be partakers of the divine
nature, having escaped the corruption that is in the
world through lust. **But also for this very** reason,
giving all diligence, add to your faith virtue, to virtue
knowledge, to knowledge self-control, to self-control
perseverance, to perseverance godliness, to godliness
brotherly kindness, and to brotherly kindness love.
For if these things are yours and abound, you will be
neither barren nor unfruitful in the knowledge of our
Lord Jesus Christ (emphasis added).

- What is "the very reason" for being diligent Peter
  alludes to?

- How are the outward manifestations of our
  inward faith a way of worship?

5. Read Luke 11:1–4.

Now it came to pass, as He was praying in a certain
place, when He ceased, that one of His disciples
said to Him, "Lord, teach us to pray, as John also
taught his disciples." So He said to them, "When
you pray, say:

Our Father in heaven,
Hallowed be Your name.
Your kingdom come.
Your will be done
On earth as it is in heaven.
Give us day by day our daily bread.
And forgive us our sins,
For we also forgive everyone who is indebted
to us.
And do not lead us into temptation,
But deliver us from the evil one.

In addition to outward behavior that reflects an inward faith, prayer is another way we worship the Lord. There is no right or wrong way to pray when our prayers derive from a sincere heart. The Lord, at the request of the disciples, did give us a model prayer.

- What are some of the key words that demonstrate this prayer is one of worship?

6. Read Luke 18.

- What two types of prayer are described in this parable?

- Do these prayers demonstrate a heart that worships?

- Why or why not?

7. Read Psalm 116:1–2.

I love the LORD, because He has heard
My voice *and* my supplications.

Because He has inclined His ear to me,
Therefore I will call *upon Him* as long as I live.

- According to these verses, why does the Psalmist love the Lord?

- Is his worship a response? An Action? Both?

8. Read Psalm 116:12–13.

   What shall I render to the LORD
   For all His benefits toward me?
   I will take up the cup of salvation,
   And call upon the name of the Lord.

   - How does the Psalmist plan to repay the Lord for his goodness?

   - Can we earn our salvation?

9. Read Psalm 139:13–14.

   For You formed my inward parts; You covered me
   in my mother's womb.
   I will praise You, for I am fearfully and
   wonderfully made;
   Marvelous are Your works,
   And that my soul knows very well.

   - According to these verses, what does the Psalmist praise the Lord for?

- How often should we worship the Lord?

- What gets in your way of experiencing and knowing God's love for you?

10. For the following references, consider for what and why we should be excited? In what way can we share this "good news"?

And because you are sons, God has sent forth the Spirit of His Son into your hearts, crying out, "Abba, Father!" (Galatians 4:6)

If we confess our sins, He is faithful and just to forgive us our sins and to cleanse us from all unrighteousness. (1 John 1:9)

And He Himself is the propitiation for our sins, and not for ours only but also for the whole world. (1 John 2:2 .

This I recall to my mind,
Therefore I have hope.
Through the LORD's mercies we are not consumed,
Because His compassions fail not.
They are new every morning;
Great is Your faithfulness.
Though He causes grief,
Yet He will show compassion
According to the multitude of His mercies.
(Lamentations 3:21–23, 32)

"I, even I, am He who blots out your transgressions
for My own sake;
And I will not remember your sins."
(Isaiah 43:25)

Chapter Three—Called to be Different

> We have more faith in what we imitate than in what we originate.... We are what other people say we are. We know ourselves chiefly by hearsay.—Bruce Lee, Martial Arts/Actor

God calls his salt to be special, pure people.

Most of humankind is born with an innate spiritual longing. We feel empty and incomplete without something beyond the nitty-gritty of food, shelter, and clothing. And with no direction or purpose, we are lost.

If not for the intervention of the Holy Spirit, the human experience would be in constant search to satisfy a lust for which there is no fulfillment apart from God. Sadly for some, this vague longing often leads to addiction of some kind.

Men try to fill the void through various means. They mistakenly believe drug use, gambling, pornography, and other addictive behaviors will fill that empty spot. Others seek power, wealth, or fame to fill the vacant place in their soul. Still others fill the dearth of satisfaction through self-sacrifice, good deeds through selfish pursuit rather than a natural extension of Christ's love within.

Even the world's vinegar recognizes the dangers in lust for lust's sake.

> We will crave that which our heart thinks it wants. Money never made a man happy yet, nor will it. There is nothing in its nature to produce happiness. The more a man has, the more he wants. Instead of filling a vacuum, it makes one. — Benjamin Franklin

OUR NATURE BEFORE CHRIST

The New Testament is filled with descriptions of our old human nature ... our vinegar ... before we received Christ. Before we received Christ, we possessed a nature contrary to God's good intentions.

AIMLESS

Without a clear direction, people tend to wander ... perhaps not even aware that they are searching for something. They look to the world's heroes as models of desirability. They don't really know what they seek, for they are merely parroting what others have purported as good. The sad truth is, the more we strive to reach an indefinable goal, the more dissatisfied we become.

BLIND

There are many instances where Jesus opened the eyes of the blind. In one such account, (Matthew 9:27– 30) two men followed after Jesus, begging for Christ's mercy. He responded by asking them, "Do you believe I can?" When they affirmed their faith, they were healed. Freedom from blindness begins with faith.

Before we received Christ, we adopted the world's values of pride, selfishness, power, and wealth. We justified our actions according to this skewered perception, the ilk of our spiritual blindness. An old English proverb states, "None so blind as those who will not see." Some choose to remain in their blindness because they refuse to acknowledge their need, they want nothing different, or believe things cannot be different.

UNGODLY

The world does place some value on morality, and those who follow a code of conduct do not see themselves as ungodly. These people believe the "decent" folk still outnumber those who pursue decadence.

Many do care about other people and are capable of showing great personal sacrifice apart from a position of faith. So what is meant by "ungodly?" Simply put, ungodly is the opposite of godly. No human, regardless of their best efforts to live a clean and wholesome life, can measure up to God's holiness.

We are ungodly by virtue of the human estate. Apart from Christ, any righteousness is self-driven rather than God imbued. Yet God commands of his salt:

> You shall be holy; for I *am* holy. (Leviticus 11:44)

For the believer, holiness is an attitude ... a desire to be godly. We will be most like those with whom we spend the most time. The more time we spend with him, the more our actions, thoughts, and desires become like his.

SHAMELESS

The world excuses mistakes and deems guilt as a bad word. We look outward for blame. In the musical, *West Side Story*, the Jets sing a satirical song to an absent Officer Krupke explaining they really aren't to blame for their behavior. After all, their delinquency is because they are simply misunderstood.

Our human condition leaves us insensitive to sin. We excuse our behaviors as "no one is perfect." That is truth. The difference between the unbeliever and the believer is the believer recognizes the fault, confesses it, and restores their relationship with the Father. The believer cannot rest until he has surrendered the recognized weakness to God.

Whereas the unbeliever does not sense a need to "get it right." They will justify their actions through a worldly standard. "Do to others as they do to you" "revenge is sweet" "you only live once" "I'm not hurting anyone, so what's the harm?"

INDECENT

In today's cultural climate, little seems to shock anyone. All we have to do is look around. Today's world view is anything goes—everything is acceptable as long as it gives pleasure. Few care about the surge in sexual content for children's programing. Vulgarity without apology is everywhere. Believers are bombarded with these messages of indecency. They are told it's okay because these images are only expressing what is normal or natural.

The Holy Spirit convicts believers of our errors, our less than holy conduct, and our impure attitudes. Rather than a lack of shame spiraling us into denial and unchanged practices, the Holy Spirit helps us gain a new outlook and encourages different actions.

GREED

Our culture glories in accumulation. We are a culture of addiction. If not drugs, then something else. A recent news report stated online shopping addiction is a disease that is becoming epidemic. Some are addicted to exercise. The internet has provided all sorts of avenues to feed any appetite. Gambling websites, gaming websites, pornography—whatever can be imagined is available at a click of a button and emptying of our wallets.

Sadly, these satisfactions are temporary, at best. If the experience titillates, we strive to repeat the high. More and more is needed to achieve the original exultation or feel-good emotion. Even after the experience fails to satisfy as the first time, we keep returning to the habit in hopes of achieving once-felt euphoria.

The believer's joy is in the Lord. When we seek him, we are never disappointed or feeling empty and unfulfilled.

ANGER

The world tells us retaliation is okay. Harboring anger in our hearts is viewed as justified, perhaps even righteous indignation. Turning the other cheek is viewed as being weak. If someone slaps us across the cheek, we turn with both fists raised. And the world glorifies this as assertiveness. We love folks who have 'tude.

When we receive Christ, our new heart will desire to be like the one who saved us. Our minds become as his, an attitudinal change overriding our actions. Through the indwelling of the Spirit, our minds adapt a new way of thinking—a new way of processing our environment and the stimuli around us. Anger is replaced by compassion, love, and understanding.

> This I say, therefore, and testify in the Lord, that you should no longer walk as the rest of the Gentiles walk, in the futility of their mind, having their understanding darkened, being alienated from the life of God, because of the ignorance that is in them, because of the blindness of their heart; who, being past feeling, have given themselves over to lewdness, to work all uncleanness with greediness. But you have not so learned Christ, if indeed you have heard Him and have been taught by Him, as the truth is in Jesus: that you put off, concerning your former conduct, the old man which grows corrupt according to the deceitful lusts, and be renewed in the spirit of your mind, and that you put on the new man which was created according to God, in true righteousness and holiness. (Ephesians 4:17–24)

THE NATURE GOD INTENDS

Before he spoke the world into creation, God purposed for those who would come to him to be without sin, blameless. And since sin entered the world through one man, Adam, sin is defeated by one man, Jesus Christ (Romans 5:17). Christ conquered sin allowing us to achieve blamelessness—not of our own volition—but made possible through his sacrifice and through the gift of the Holy Spirit. He who washes us also purifies us, allowing us to stand before God clean, whole, and his child. With a new heart and a new mind, made in his image.

God has intended from the beginning to provide a new covenant, imperishable, and written on hearts rather than on tablets and accomplished through the work of Christ.

In that He says, "'A new covenant," He has made the first obsolete. Now what is becoming obsolete and growing old is ready to vanish away. (Hebrews 8:13)

This new heart and new mind shape us into the image of God, so our lives will reflect God's nature. This we cannot do through effort. A new heart and new mind can only come through his grace and the gift of the Holy Spirit. A desire to become more like the living God.

This is not only the believer's desire but is also God's desire for his salt.

If you're like me, being recreated in God's image seems impossible. He's holy. He's perfect. How can a mortal like me be like him? Yet, God says we are and should be.

SELF-IMPROVEMENT VS GOD'S IMPROVEMENT

Self-help books are in abundance—books sure to instruct us on anything from best love practices to how to stay glamorous in old age. Books to improve our self-confidence—how to see ourselves as winners. Books on losing weight and staying fit.

This self-seeking can be insidious. The vinegary philosophies can easily corrode our perspective as God's salt, for these so-called helps are focused on the temporal—fleeting things having little to do with being holy or seeking to reflect the image of God stamped within us.

The world is full of advice as to how we should look. What clothes will bring out the person hidden deep inside. How we should wear our hair to enhance our best facial traits, and maybe hide the ones that are not so flattering. The world tells us how much we should weigh to be a healthy and attractive person.

The world teaches if we eat the right foods, get the right kind of exercise, wear the right clothes we'll be successful and content. Such a view does more to harm self-esteem than build a positive self-image. We constantly struggle to become the image of what others have divined is right for us not what God has purposed.

The world wants us to refashion ourselves according to humanity's vision of what is good. In order to fit in, to look like, and project the image the world wants us to be requires constant updating.

Salt finds its worth in our position as God's child, a position not based upon achievement but on God's mercy. When we come to him in faith, trusting in his mercy and finding salvation, God casts our sins into the deepest part of his forgetfulness. They are erased as if we'd never erred. We don't forget our past, but God does.

> Or do you not know that your body is the temple of the Holy Spirit who is in you, whom you have from God, and you are not your own? For you were bought at a price; therefore glorify God in your body and in your spirit, which are God's. (1 Corinthians 6:19–20)

Our actions will spill out from a new self-image. We want to please God instead of others. Such a changed view, moving from vinegar to salt, is freeing because our confidence develops from a knowledge of whose we are:

> Follow God's example, therefore, as dearly loved children and walk in the way of love, just as Christ loved us and gave himself up for us as a fragrant offering and sacrifice to God. (Ephesians 5:1–2 NIV)

Our new self, made in God's image, begins when we come to faith in Christ. Only then can God infuse us with his holiness and begin crafting us in his image.

> That, however, is not the way of life you learned when you heard about Christ and were taught in him in accordance with the truth that is in Jesus. You were taught, with regard to your former way of life, to put off your old self, which is being corrupted by its deceitful desires, to be made new in the attitude of your minds;

and to put on the new self, created to be like God in true righteousness and holiness. (Ephesians 4:20–24 NIV)

THE NATURAL DESIRE FOR CHANGE

Though I resist change, I know doing so is inevitable. I know I'd rather not ride in a horse and buggy or even drive the old cars I grew up with no air conditioning or heaters. In one old car I drove, I had the choice of heat or defrost. I'm grateful for the changes technology has brought to our lives. As a writer, I'm grateful I no longer have to decipher my own handwriting.

All the messages bombarding me through television and the internet beg me to change, to conform to the manufacturer's idea of what I should look like. All too often, I succumb to the fashionable, to the convenient, to the latest "must have" device.

Our biological construction requires us to change. We create more than 200 billion new cells daily. I've learned to breathe is to change.

But to change into what?

There is a lesson to be learned from studying the caterpillar. When nature dictates, it unconsciously creates a cocoon and hibernates. When it emerges, the caterpillar is no longer what it once was. It has been transformed into something beautiful, a testament to the God who created it. Without change, the caterpillar would always remain a furry little creature stuck to the ground, inching its way through a limited world.

If change is a natural byproduct of our physical world, how much more is change a part of our spiritual world? How much more does God want us to become the product of his design?

To breathe in God's Spirit invites a metamorphosis. The more we know of God, the more we want to be like him. But how do we know what we should change in order to be a good Christian? How do we implement the change?

WHO PUT THE VINEGAR IN THE SALT
"THE MAN IN THE MIRROR"

The popular song by the late Michael Jackson, portrays a man who is cognizant of humanity's sufferings and realizes if the world is to change, the change must first begin with him. Almost right. At least from a humanistic point of view. Even the vinegar of the world recognizes effective change must be intrinsic. There must be something willful in our transformation.

Most of us would like to be better people—kinder, gentler, and more compassionate. Many of us strive toward that goal. I know I want to project an image of goodness. The momentary pride I might feel by accomplishing something worthwhile in the world's esteem is soon replaced by the harsh reality of my imperfect self. Sin rears, and I fall flat on my face, stung with the reality of my own inability to "do Christian."

We'll look at the attributes of victorious living in the second part of the book. For now, let's explore the beauty of the Christian life. Not a doing but a being. What if the reflection God wants us to see in our mirrors is not our own image, but Christ in us?

THE NATURE OF GOD

We are told in the first few chapters of Genesis humankind was created in God's image. Theologians present many ideas as to what this means. As a parent, I've gained a few glimpses as to the possible implications of what being made in God's image might include.

Our biological children resemble us. In addition, our children, or the young minds we influence, are inheritors of our philosophies, our values, our examples. Our natural inclination is to want our children, those under our care, to adopt the same values we hold dear. Some parents might discourage their children from following in their footsteps.

They may not want their offspring to make the same bad choices they made. Either way, we have an image in our minds of what we want our children to become. In our human efforts, we attempt to shape these young lives to be happy and productive members of society. We guide them toward those goals as best we can.

If we in our imperfect world desire good things for our children, how much more does God want us, his salt, to experience the fullness of him, through a changed heart and mind.

Being tossed from the Garden of Eden did not negate our physiological connection to God. Every human tribe and culture, past and present, has developed a system of morality and a way to judge its denizens accordingly—even idol worshippers or those who claim there is no god.

Ancient Israel had the advantage of the best code of ethics ever. Yet they struggled to be obedient, and their failure to live up to the standard God set for them led to devastating consequences. Even within God's harsh judgment against them, his compassion and love for his people was evident. His constant prophecy was to shape them. "I will be their God, and they will be my people."

He had a plan—a plan to put his image upon their hearts so a desire to do good would be an outflow from an inner transformation.

> Behold, I will do a new thing,
> Now it shall spring forth;
> Shall you not know it?
> I will even make a road in the wilderness
> And rivers in the desert. (Isaiah 43:19)

> I will give you a new heart and put a new spirit within you; I will take the heart of stone out of your flesh and give you a heart of flesh. (Ezekiel 36:26)

Paul struggled with a human desire to be all the law required, to live according to the ethical tradition, a

Pharisee above all other Pharisees, a student of the most renowned Hebrew scholars. Though passionate for righteousness, the strength of his passion came from a belief good resulted from man's self-determination. In his mistaken zeal, he persecuted the new church. How could he abide this heretical devotion to someone whom he believed could not be the Messiah?

Until he had a personal encounter with Jesus, Paul didn't realize the futility of trying to live by a moral code without a personal relationship with the author of that code. If so, the law would have been all that was needed.

> For we know that the law is spiritual, but I am carnal, sold under sin. For what I am doing, I do not understand. For what I will to do, that I do not practice; but what I hate, that I do. If, then, I do what I will not to do, I agree with the law that it is good. But now, it is no longer I who do it, but sin that dwells in me. For I know that in me (that is, in my flesh) nothing good dwells; for to will is present with me, but how to perform what is good I do not find. For the good that I will to do, I do not do; but the evil I will not to do, that I practice. Now if I do what I will not to do, it is no longer I who do it, but sin that dwells in me. (Romans 7:14–20)

But humanistic morality, vinegar, is but a shadow of what God can do when he is the instrument of change—when he refashions us into his image as we were once created.

To live as salt requires a comprehension of what it means to be God's child. He has invested himself into us in order for us to live according to his attributes, not by imposed standards set by a world in opposition to God, rather by a code that is God installed.

We do not argue with moral accolades or when worldly philosophers tout the values of forgiveness, generosity, and marital faithfulness. The Christian embraces these tenets as well. The difference between salt and vinegar is the degree of relativity we place on these values.

God Imprints His Nature on Our Hearts

The world's microscope is tainted and inconsistent. Values change according to the most popular ideology of the day. All we need to do is to read a few headlines to get a good picture of what extremes the world will go to for compliance to a fad ideology, justifying violence as a means to an end. This pattern puts humankind at the center rather than God, allowing for conduct to change according to what is expedient.

The world says, "love your neighbor" but not if your neighbor treats you unfairly. Jesus teaches we should turn the other cheek. The world says forgiveness is good, but you can't forgive someone who doesn't want to be forgiven. Jesus says you should forgive others as God has forgiven you—unconditionally. These divine attributes can only come from God who imprints his image on our hearts.

For Further Study or Group Discussion

1. Read Genesis 25.

   • What did Esau trade for his favorite stew?

   • Esau rejected God's blessing, then became angry that his birthright was indeed taken from him. Why are we surprised when bad things happen because of our choices?

   • How is this different for the believer?

2. Read Jeremiah 24:6–7.

> For I will set My eyes on them for good, and I will bring them back to this land; I will build them and not pull them down, and I will plant them and not pluck them up. Then I will give them a heart to know Me, that I am the LORD; and they shall be My people, and I will be their God, for they shall return to Me with their whole heart.

- What guiding principle does God desire for his people?

- How can they know what is right and good?

3. Read Jeremiah 29:11–13.

> For I know the thoughts that I think toward you, says the LORD, thoughts of peace and not of evil, to give you a future and a hope. Then you will call upon Me and go and pray to Me, and I will listen to you. And you will seek Me and find Me, when you search for Me with all your heart.

- What does God intend for his children?

- When will his children find him?

4. Read Luke 6:43–45.

> For a good tree does not bear bad fruit, nor does a bad tree bear good fruit. For every tree is known by its own fruit. For men do not gather figs from thorns,

nor do they gather grapes from a bramble bush. A good man out of the good treasure of his heart brings forth good; and an evil man out of the evil treasure of his heart brings forth evil. For out of the abundance of the heart his mouth speaks.

- Where do good deeds spring from?

- Where do evil deeds spring from? Why?

- What gives precedence to our thoughts and ultimately what we say and do?

5. Read Romans 12:1–2.

I beseech you therefore, brethren, by the mercies of God, that you present your bodies a living sacrifice, holy, acceptable to God, which is your reasonable service. And do not be conformed to this world, but be transformed by the renewing of your mind, that you may prove what is that good and acceptable and perfect will of God.

- Look up the meaning of conformity

- Look up the meaning of transformation.

- How are these different?

- How is transformation achieved?

The Lord provides a Spirit of renewal, a new heart and a new mind through the work of the Holy Spirit. Conformity is an adherence to a code of conduct ... for the Israelites, the law of Moses.

6. Read 2 Corinthians 5:17.

    Therefore, if anyone is in Christ, he is a new creation; old things have passed away; behold, all things have become new.

    • What must pass away in order for all things to become new?

    • What old things are you hanging on to?

    • Do these old things prevent you from finding the newness God has in store for you?

7. Read Colossians 3.

    • In what way do these verses express a new way or a new mindset in our worship and relationship to the Lord?

8. Read 1 Peter 1:22.

    Since you have purified your souls in obeying the truth through the Spirit in sincere love of the brethren, love one another fervently with a pure heart.

    • What gives us the power to love others with a pure heart?

9. Read 1 Peter 2:4–5.

Coming to Him as to a living stone, rejected indeed by men, but chosen by God and precious, you also, as living stones, are being built up a spiritual house, a holy priesthood, to offer up spiritual sacrifices acceptable to God through Jesus Christ.

- How are believers living stones?

- In what way are we rejected by men?

- Why are we chosen by God?

- To what is God building us up to be? What does God what us to sacrifice?

10. Read 1 Peter 2:9–10.

But you are a chosen generation, a royal priesthood, a holy nation, His own special people, that you may proclaim the praises of Him who called you out of darkness into His marvelous light; who once were not a people but are now the people of God, who had not obtained mercy but now have obtained mercy.

- What does it mean to be a "chosen generation?"

- What does God want us to proclaim?

- God has brought us out of darkness to what?

- What did we obtain that we had not obtained before?

Chapter Four—Called for a Purpose

If we have never had the experience of taking our commonplace religious shoes off our commonplace religious feet and getting rid of all the undue familiarity with which we approach God, it is questionable whether we have ever stood in His presence. —Oswald Chambers

Earlier, I mentioned one reason we are salt is to let our lives be an example to a hurting world—a reflection of what God can do—to be a light in the darkness so others can find their way to God.

> The Spirit of the Lord GOD is upon Me,
> Because the LORD has anointed Me
> To preach good tidings to the poor;
> He has sent Me to heal the brokenhearted,
> To proclaim liberty to the captives,
> And the opening of the prison to those who are bound;
> To proclaim the acceptable year of the LORD,
> And the day of vengeance of our God;
> To comfort all who mourn,
> To console those who mourn in Zion,
> To give them beauty for ashes,
> The oil of joy for mourning,
> The garment of praise for the spirit of heaviness;
> That they may be called trees of righteousness,
> The planting of the LORD, that He may be glorified.
> (Isaiah 61:1–3)

As our new hearts and new minds help us to be more like him, we develop a desire to let others know they too can be free from the bondage of sin. We are salt to bring comfort to those who are hurting.

CALLED TO BLOOM

God also transforms his salt for purpose and design. When we accept him as our Lord and Savior, we enter into a relationship with God. He is no longer a someone we have heard about or have a little knowledge of. He is in us, and we are in him. We become his oaks of righteousness.

Do you ever think of yourself as a tree—tall and straight and fully adorned in green leaves? Once we were poor, despairing, prisoners, and lost. God wants so much more for us. He desires to make us strong, straight, and able to endure.

Whether our circumstances are of our own making, a calamity or catastrophe beyond our imaginings, or because of humankind's rebellion, I believe God wants to make the dark places light, satiate the hungry, and set the captive free.

I believe God intimately knows our deepest fears, sins, and the ugly places in our hearts. He wants to purge these rotting spots to make us bloom with fruit. Why are we so slow to respond to his pruning?

THE PATH TO PURPOSE

The Lord asked the paralytic man at the wading pool a seemingly foolish question:

"Wilt thou be whole?" (John 5:6 KJV).

If he were cured, his life would change dramatically. He had to decide whether to walk in newness, to find a purpose for his life and a new direction, or cling to the security of the old. Healing and freedom would catapult him into the unfamiliar.

Perhaps that is why the path to repentance and salvation is so narrow (Matthew 7:13). This path is an entrance into a vast unknown and few dare to choose to travel unknown territory. While our destination is assured, the ruts, curves, and byways may not be clearly laid out in advance. For many believers, the journey from purposelessness to purpose is frightening.

To use us, God must reshape us. To be his feet, we must put on new shoes—those he has predestined for us to wear. Sometimes, this is a metamorphosis as we continue to learn more and more about the Lord. We can be sure, God will finish what he has started within us to put us on the path to our purpose, our ministry.

I am reminded of a children's chorus from many years ago. The song reminds us our character speaks so loudly sometimes the world cannot hear our words. We drown our witness in noise and arguments and destroy the very mission we have undertaken—to spread the good news.

God has called us to be trees, not megaphones.

ACCEPTING GOD'S DESIGN

Perhaps another reason we fail to realize our ministry as believers is our constant argument with God as to the process he is undertaking to recreate us to be usable.

Consider the giraffe.

Logically, the giraffe should not survive. It is an awkward animal and too gangly. Because its head is so far removed from the heart, by reason, the giraffe should collapse from the pull of gravity. But the Creator designed the giraffe's physiology to support its unusual height and build. Instead of low blood pressure like most mammals, the giraffe has high blood pressure, normalized by its superior heart construction.

I forget I am made exactly as God chose me to be, though often his design for me makes no sense. He calls me to look at the creatures of the land and sea. And he reminds me each creation bears its own mark upon the earth, though its feats seem impossible.

How can anything as big as a whale propel itself through the water and into the air before splashing back into the ocean?

What we fail to realize is how God has designed all living things according to his good pleasure.

Like humans, some creatures tend to be dominant on one side more than the other. Some fish tend to use one eye more than another as they search for predators. Since there are more right-eyed fish, they swim with the school to avoid danger. One would think the left-eyed fish could not survive. Left-eyed fish flee in the opposite direction, and their erratic behavior confuses their enemies.

I imagine God revels in their flight.

Cicadas are another perplexing creation. The first time I saw them, I wondered why God designed such annoying creatures. They come out of hibernation every ten to seventeen years, depending upon their species, for the sole purpose of chirping and breeding.

We had come south for the dedication of one of our grandchildren. The front lawn of the church was carpeted with the clamoring insects. Their "song" was so loud, we could barely hear our own voices.

I felt God reminding me: "Hear that. These creatures are praising me. I love to hear their song."

Only humans, those he made in his image, defy God's design. We shake a fist at the Creator and say, "Why did you make me this way?" Does the giraffe ask God why he isn't like the horse? Does the left-eyed fish tell God he wants to swim with the right-eyed schools? Does the whale take issue with the Almighty for the ups and downs of its life? Does the cicada stop chirping because his life span is so short?

Years ago, teachers were advised to retrain children who tried to write left-handed. They believed allowing this physiological aberration would impede the child's ability to read.

Psychologists now believe left-handedness, in actuality, provides an advantage. This is seen in the sports world by legends such as golfers Bubba Watson and Phil Mickelson, baseball's legend Babe Ruth, basketball's Bill Russell, soccer's Lionel Messi, and tennis great Martina Navratilova. Some studies indicate left-handed people tend to have higher intellectual capacity and think outside the norm, as evidenced by Albert Einstein, Isaac Newton, and Benjamin Franklin. An internet search reveals many famous lefties from all walks of life. These people learned to embrace their difference, to see their less than common hand dominance, not as abnormal, rather as opportunity.

I wonder if the church has not become like the well-meaning teachers who believed left-handedness should be discouraged. Do we sometimes chastise fellow believers because they think or act outside established church protocols? Do we sometimes think the believer who swims away from the school of the scripturally learned is lacking in faith? Perhaps God has designed some of us to stretch our long necks and feed from the topmost branches or push from the depths into the air, spouting with enthusiasm. Perhaps, like the oddities of his creation, God has instilled all believers with a unique stamp for his good pleasure.

God's Creation Song

Is our quest to conform to standardized observances of our worship and community of believers a thinly disguised resistance against God's reshaping his church to be the hands and feet of his word to the world? Just as God's creation is vastly diverse, so is the church. The Psalmist understood the unique character of humankind above all of God's creation.

I will praise You, for I am fearfully and wonderfully made;

Marvelous are Your works,
And that my soul knows very well.
(Psalm 139:14)

God did not create the world to be empty, rather to be inhabited, to have function for his good pleasure. When we come to him, he creates a new spirit within us not only to serve this world he loves but to allow our lives to be the song that gives him praise.

Yet, we tend to grow impatient while we are in God's cocoon.

I moved into a new home before all the finishing touches could be completed. The thing about occupying a home while doing renovations is that you readily adjust to the less desirable. Reconstruction takes energy—energy that becomes quickly depleted with the demands of everyday life. I had a book launch to prepare for and deadlines were looming. The mundane took precedence over the permanent.

As a temporary measure, I hung up sheets for window coverings until I could figure out what to do next. Unfortunately, the longer I postponed making improvements, the more content I became with the ugliness surrounding me. Satisfactory became good enough. To the point, I stopped believing beautiful could be possible.

My sister-in-law served as my interior design consultant and, in her view, satisfactory was unacceptable. She lavished me with home gifts sure to inspire the dormant decorator within. Even with my cheerleader beside me, the process was tedious. I thought I'd scream if I had to do one more project. When she brought in a third set of patio drapes, the first two not meeting her expectations, I drooped in pain. Not again! Hadn't I already made enough adjustment? What was already there seemed sufficient. Why go through more hassle?

"Just try them," she urged.

Then I remembered: Marianne asked me to do this out of love. Her knowledge of interior design far exceeded mine. She was confident the improvement would bring me great joy.

I mustered the will to hang the drapes. When I viewed the results, I wept in thanksgiving. What joy! What beauty! A melody I had not expected. More than I could ever have imagined. The rich chocolate color was exactly what was needed to pull the room together in purpose and design—undeserved comfort in my moments of solitude. Pleasure I would have missed if I had not let go of the status quo.

Don't we sometimes approach our spiritual development with the same disinterest? We are satisfied to sing "Twinkle, Twinkle, Little Star" for our entire lives when God wants us to learn opera. God does not withhold any good thing from his child. He has a vision for our lives, and what He sees is best for us. How happy we'd be if we would allow him to complete what he has begun. How sad that we have become satisfied with the mundane, the plunking of repetitive notes instead of yearning to perform an aria.

Accepting good enough means we don't allow God to complete the process of renewal—a painful process at times, disruptive to our routines, and difficult to learn. We become so absorbed by the status quo, we no longer expect or even desire God's infilling. How much he wants to make us into a symphony, but we're content to remain an unfinished melody.

We are wise to remember: God loves us.

He knows us better than we know ourselves.

His design for our lives is more than we could ever hope or dream.

> I thank my God upon every remembrance of you, always in every prayer of mine making request for you all with joy, for your fellowship in the gospel from the first day until now, being confident of this very thing, that He who has begun a good work in you will complete it until the day of Jesus Christ. (Philippians 1:3–6)

PURPOSE IN UNCERTAINTY

Oswald Chambers suggests there are three aspects of the spiritual life: worship, waiting, and work. He often writes Christians think these states work in harmony with the others. In essence: we worship and work while waiting, we wait and work while worshiping, we wait and worship while working. This sounds contradictory, but this is the way the Spirit works.

Maybe we tire of the process. Or maybe we slip back into the old and familiar because we're not sure of God's direction. Waiting, worshiping, and work becomes tedious. Harder still is communing and obeying God in a state of flux. We believe God has a plan, but he seems slow in revealing the plan to us. The expectation and frustration in the expectation is not unique. Most believers feel this way at some time or another. Does God really have a purpose in keeping me in the dark?

After what I thought would be a routine mammogram, the radiologist said, "There are spots. One of them is highly suspicious. You need to have this taken care of right away." The urgency in the warning prompted me to act quickly.

While I waited for results, of course I felt anxious. Anxiety is the natural human response to uncertainty. Yet the more God reminded me I was his child, and he'd be with me regardless of the outcome, my pleading became prayers of praise. I would not face this alone. He reassured me there was a reason for this event in my life. If he so allowed, he would then provide the strength and grace not only to endure, but also to bloom—regardless of the outcome.

And so I moved forward in worship and work while I waited. When the news came the tumor was indeed cancerous. God had already prepared my heart. Yes ... I cried, but God wiped my tears with a spiritual handkerchief and sent me on my way with a hug. "You'll be fine," he promised.

Throughout the course of treatment, he occupied my mind with book contracts and filled my spirit with laughter. I make a very funny bald person.

Waiting need not be a time of stagnation, frozen because of our anxiety, hounding heaven with the question, "What purpose is there in this trial, God?"

In the song, "While I'm Waiting," by John Walker, made famous by the movie *Fireproof*, the writer states he will worship while he's waiting. He will do so by remaining hopeful, even though he is hurting. He will worship in waiting by moving forward, serving, loving, and doing the things he knows God expects from him.

Joyce Meyer lists two important aspects of waiting on God:

1. Expect he has heard your prayer and will answer and
2. Be eager with faith.

"It's just like when a woman is expecting a baby," she says. "Even though she can't see the baby, she knows the baby is there. She prepares and keeps busy. Nine months can be a very long time if she were to simply sit in a chair and do nothing until the baby comes."

Faith prompts us to action, to praise, to purpose. Doubt paralyzes. Our service and continued commitment during this time of uncertainty is our song of praise.

> Therefore the LORD will wait, that He may be gracious to you; And therefore He will be exalted, that He may have mercy on you. For the LORD is a God of justice; Blessed are all those who wait for Him. (Isaiah 30:18)

FINDING PURPOSE THOUGH SUFFERING

We can't fathom what purpose God can bring through our suffering, especially while we are in the midst of trial. Sometimes we must worship, work, and wait through tragedy. During these times of grief, we want God to purge the pain, not use it to shape us.

In the book, *Song for Sarah*, Paula D'Arcy chronicles her grief through a disappointing pregnancy. When she first learned she'd have a child, she wrote letters to her unborn whom she named Sarah. Later, Paula learned her baby was stillborn. In her deepest sorrow she continued to write to Sarah. Paula spilled out her honest anger and resentment toward God. "Where are you?" she asked. Yet while waiting, she moved forward in worship and work. When the day of her delivery came, she felt God's power and deliverance from fear. He had never been far away but made his presence the most powerful when she needed him the most. Later, her story brought solace to thousands.

God's purpose in allowing suffering can be two-fold. To let us know that he is with us in these hardest times. Also, to prepare us to be a comfort to others. Having experienced the power of God's presence, we can then counsel someone else in like circumstances.

In a TV special about the long-running television show *Jeopardy*, Alex Trebek, the long-time host of the show, before he died, talked about his pancreatic cancer diagnosis. He read a letter to his staff received by a fan after Alex shared his symptoms on one of the episodes. The fan told Alex how her husband noticed he had similar symptoms and went to the doctor. Fortunately, the man's cancer was found early enough to be given a good prognosis. The fan stated Alex's honesty about his illness probably saved her husband's life.

"How about that," Alex said. "I was able to save a life through my suffering. That makes me feel good."

Paul and Silas found themselves in the deepest part of a prison. Perhaps they felt abandoned and forgotten. (Acts 16). Perhaps they wondered what purpose could come from this detour when their desire was to spread the gospel. Yet, they faced the hardest part of waiting by praising God with expectation.

WHO PUT THE VINEGAR IN THE SALT
FINDING PURPOSE THROUGH GROWTH

God's purpose and design for us also includes our growing deeper in knowledge and wisdom.

Whenever God chides me to "be patient for wisdom," my mind instantly returns to a training camp graduation at Ft. Jackson, South Carolina on a hot July day. The temperature soared to 95 degrees, and it was only nine o'clock in the morning. Hailing from the North, these blistering temperatures challenged the very act of breathing. The beads of perspiration dripping from my forehead blurred my vision somewhat, but I was certain my son stood on the end of the third row among all the other sons and daughters dressed in familiar drab greens. The soldiers stood in perfect formation, even my son Jim. There were many mothers assembled, but I knew I was one of the proudest. The journey to this time and place had been difficult for the both of us.

When he announced his decision to enter the Army, mouths remained agape for several seconds. Of all the choices available to him, this was the least expected. Learning to surrender unquestioning obedience to less than perfect human beings would prove to be his ultimate test.

Jim could have authored a book, *The Art of Passive Resistance for Children*. His developmental years were spent in passive rebellion, authority to be challenged at every turn. Like the mountain, he would not be moved. He was Defiance in the flesh. He challenged every form and creative measure of discipline I could invent.

Feeling Jim's non-compliant nature had a direct relationship to some motherly deficiency, I set out on a course of correction. I had grown weary of the countless parent-teacher conferences ending in the insinuation I needed to take parenting classes. I was a professional social worker. Certainly, I was smarter than a nine-year-old.

I thought back on those many battles. No creative instruction I mustered helped until one day I realized the secret to Jim's motivation. He only changed behaviors that created problems for him. As his wisdom and understanding grew, his behavior changed.

God reminded me of the following verse:

> If any of you lacks wisdom, let him ask of God, who gives to all liberally and without reproach, and it will be given to him. (James 1:5)

I watched my stubborn son move methodically through his drills and beamed with pride, glad for the gift of him and for the special qualities God gave him, assured he would complete the good work God had begun in his heart.

The true purpose of spiritual wisdom and understanding is to enable the Christian to walk worthy of the Lord, to realize their full potential in their relationship with him. This was Paul's prayer for the saints:

> For this reason we also, since the day we heard it, do not cease to pray for you, and to ask that you may be filled with the knowledge of His will in all wisdom and spiritual understanding; that you may walk worthy of the Lord, fully pleasing Him, being fruitful in every good work and increasing in the knowledge of God; strengthened with all might, according to His glorious power, for all patience and longsuffering with joy; giving thanks to the Father who has qualified us to be partakers of the inheritance of the saints in the light. (Colossians 1:9–12)

I'm not very good with a cell phone. Bad eyes and fat fingers. I resisted getting a cell phone until I had to travel to see my daughter who was going into premature labor. My husband could not travel with me and wanted me to have the ability to keep in touch and a little protection as I drove the long distance by myself.

I got so I liked having a cell phone.

Then texting became popular.

Oh my!

But the more I used the device, the more proficient I became. I'm hardly an expert, but I'm certainly better than what I was.

Similarly, I despised computers until I was forced to use them at work. The more I used them, the more I liked them. We bought our first PC, and I was hooked. Then God called me to write. I was ever so grateful I had a rudimentary knowledge of the programs to help with my writing career.

Need spurred the desire to gain in wisdom and understanding and consequently changed my behavior for the better, equipping me to complete God's purpose in my life.

If God gives understanding and wisdom in our natural world, how much more will he endow in the spiritual realm.

FINDING PURPOSE THROUGH OUR GIFTS

Jesus pointed out to his disciples, perhaps when they quarreled among themselves over who was the smartest or most deserving of promotion, gifts were given for the common good of the body, to help the body grow with purpose and design (Matthew 25:14–28).

Many theologians point to this chapter to demonstrate the need to use our "talents" wisely. I also note the master knew how much to give to each servant in hopes of enlarging his kingdom. I expect he was not surprised at the lazy action of the last servant. Perhaps he was angry because he wasn't given the same as the other two.

The church today tends to value some ministries as more valuable to the church than others. Some ministries are unseen by the multitude but are necessary for church function. A greeter's hug has the potential to bless as much as a carefully rehearsed ensemble.

When my good friend had cancer, I chauffeured her two hours from home for her chemo treatments. During her time at the cancer center, I read to her from a Christian novel—a humorous chic lit with a good Christian message. She laughed ... laughter bringing healing for cancer patients. A male nurse approached me, somewhat apologetic, thanking me for reading aloud.

"I'm a pastor. I had never thought fiction could be a true ministry. I was wrong."

God can use gifts in remarkable ways.

Paul was concerned that the Corinthian church emphasized one spiritual gift over another, prompting him to write one of the most cherished chapters in the Bible, the definition of the gift of love, love demonstrated by God, love God purposes for us to imitate as we grow in wisdom and understanding (1 Corinthians 13).

> There are diversities of gifts, but the same Spirit. There are differences of ministries, but the same Lord. And there are diversities of activities, but it is the same God who works all in all. (1 Corinthians 12:4–6)

Whether wisdom, knowledge, faith power, prophecy, discernment, language and interpretation, God gives to each one as he determines for his good purpose. Though many of us will never obtain a doctorate in philosophy or religion, God will, through our continued investment in prayer, scripture reading, and personal study increase our wisdom and understanding. Not from our own power, but through God's ever-increasing bestowment. He will give us the exact measure when we need the right instruction to fulfill the purpose he has predetermined for his salt.

Solomon knew where wisdom and understanding began and instructed his son to value the wisdom God gives.

> To know wisdom and instruction,
> To perceive the words of understanding,

To receive the instruction of wisdom,
Justice, judgment, and equity;
To give prudence to the simple,
To the young man knowledge and discretion—
A wise man will hear and increase learning,
And a man of understanding will attain wise counsel,
To understand a proverb and an enigma,
The words of the wise and their riddles.
The fear of the LORD is the beginning of knowledge,
But fools despise wisdom and instruction.
(Proverbs 1:2–7)

The Lord continues to call his salt to seek these attributes in order to become what he has destined us to become. He has promised to give to each what is needed.

David, too, desired God's purpose in his life and trusted God's guidance.

I will run the course of Your commandments,
For You shall enlarge my heart. (Psalm 119:32)

Some translations use, "you have set my heart free." I like this thought. For increased wisdom and understanding is indeed freeing, giving us our wings when we come out of our cocoons.

We are intended to grow in our understanding of God through practice of our faith … first we crawl, then we lumber, eventually we learn to run. In Part II, we'll look at what living as salt means. Faith—hard faith, victorious faith that works.

Every newborn in our natural world has to learn to advance through life by some process in order to become a functioning adult.

In order to grow in wisdom as we find God's purpose and design for our lives, we must leave our failures behind as Paul suggests in several of his epistles. We cannot grow in our walk if we stay stuck in the mud of the past.

Therefore, leaving the discussion of the elementary principles of Christ, let us go on to perfection, not laying again the foundation of repentance from dead works and of faith toward God. (Hebrews 6:1)

FOR FURTHER STUDY OR GROUP DISCUSSION

1. Read Jeremiah 24:7.

    Then I will give them a heart to know Me, that I am the LORD; and they shall be My people, and I will be their God, for they shall return to Me with their whole heart.

    *   What is God's purpose for his salt?

    *   How does he accomplish this?

2. Read Psalm 39:4.

    LORD, make me to know my end,
    And what is the measure of my days,
    That I may know how frail I am.

    *   How does examining our days and understanding our frailty help us to find God's true purpose for our lives?

3. Read Philippians 3:13–14.

    Brethren, I do not count myself to have apprehended; but one thing I do, forgetting those things which are behind and reaching forward to those things which are ahead, I press toward the goal for the prize of the upward call of God in Christ Jesus.

- What does Paul strive to achieve?

- Why does he feel he has not yet "apprehended" this?

- How does he proceed?

- Why is forgetting those things behind important to finding our purpose in Christ?

4. Read Matthew 6:33.

   But seek first the kingdom of God and His righteousness, and all these things shall be added to you.

   - What other things will be added?

   - Why does God want us to put him first?

   - How does putting God first help us to find our purpose?

5. Read Philippians 2:12–13.

   Therefore, my beloved, as you have always obeyed, not as in my presence only, but now much more in my absence, work out your own salvation with fear and trembling; for it is God who works in you both to will and to do for His good pleasure.

   - In the preceding verses (5–11), Paul admonishes us to adopt the mind of Christ. What do you think he means by "working out your own salvation?"

   - Is this contradictory to finding salvation by faith?

   - According to verse 13, who does the work?

   - How does knowing this, help us to understand and find our purpose?

6. Read 2 Corinthians 1:20–22.

   For all the promises of God in Him are Yes, and in Him Amen, to the glory of God through us. Now He who establishes us with you in Christ and has anointed us is God, who also has sealed us and given us the Spirit in our hearts as a guarantee.

   - Do you believe God wants you to succeed? Why or why not?

   - How does God establish his purpose in us?

- What guarantee does God provide that we are called to a purpose? What purpose?

7. Read Ephesians 3: 14–19.

For this reason I bow my knees to the Father of our Lord Jesus Christ, from whom the whole family in heaven and earth is named, that He would grant you, according to the riches of His glory, to be strengthened with might through His Spirit in the inner man, that Christ may dwell in your hearts through faith; that you, being rooted and grounded in love, may be able to comprehend with all the saints what is the width and length and depth and height— to know the love of Christ which passes knowledge; that you may be filled with all the fullness of God.

- Examine the preceding verses. What does Paul mean, "for this reason?"

- Paul often referred to himself as the "greatest of sinners." While he remembered his past, he continued to press forward in faith to the purpose for which God called him. What was that purpose?

- What did Paul hope the people of Ephesus would grasp?

- How would that help them to find their purpose?

8. Read Proverbs 19:21.

There are many plans in a man's heart,
Nevertheless the LORD's counsel—that will stand.

- What human plans could detract from the Lord's purposes for us?

- Have you ever experienced a detour from your plans and later saw God's imprint in the disruption?

9. Read Isaiah 46:4, 8–11.

Even to your old age, I am He,
And even to gray hairs I will carry you!
I have made, and I will bear;
Even I will carry, and will deliver you.

Remember this, and show yourselves men;
Recall to mind, O you transgressors.
Remember the former things of old,
For I *am* God, and *there is* no other;
I am God, and *there is* none like Me,
Declaring the end from the beginning,
And from ancient times *things* that are not *yet*
done, Saying, "My counsel shall stand,
And I will do all My pleasure," Calling a bird of
prey from the east, The man who executes My
counsel, from a far country. Indeed I have spoken
it; I have purposed *it.*

- How does verse 4 compare with verses 8–10?

- How do these verses bring comfort?

- Have you ever experienced a time when remembering "the former things of old" gave you confidence God would fulfill his promise?

10. Read Proverbs 4:11–12.

> I have taught you in the way of wisdom;
> I have led you in right paths.
> When you walk, your steps will not be hindered,
> And when you run, you will not stumble.

- Who teaches us wisdom?

- What paths does God lead us on?

- What reassurance is there that God's path is the right path?

- Why do you think God sometimes does not reveal the whole plan?

Chapter Five—Called for Fellowship

> Therefore do not be unwise, but understand what the will of the Lord is. And do not be drunk with wine, in which is dissipation; but be filled with the Spirit, speaking to one another in psalms and hymns and spiritual songs, singing and making melody in your heart to the Lord, giving thanks always for all things to God the Father in the name of our Lord Jesus Christ, submitting to one another in the fear of God. (Ephesians 5:17–21)

Salt can be described as "an active element found naturally in combined form." Salt is formed by linking two separate elements together, sometimes the unthinkable and unlikely. Common table salt is formed from the union of sodium and chlorine, a poisonous substance that gives bleach its offensive odor. Yet once combined, the result is a substance that preserves and adds flavor.

THE SALT OF THE EARTH

Christ called believers "the salt of the earth."

Was he speaking this truth to individuals or to a collective group? Or both?

Does he expect believers will, like sodium and chlorine, disparate yet redeemed, bind together and form a substance to bless the world? Is Christian unity even possible?

The origins of the word community date back to the Arabic, from the word ummah, sometimes used to describe a collective nation of states. Community is also a way of life in the Israelite tradition. The word for community in Hebrew is translated "a people." From its Judaic roots, community also infused the early church. Indeed, Christendom refers to *corpus Christianum*, the Christian body—the community of all Christians.

Does this mean God intends for believers to become a community exclusive to themselves, developing their own government and way of life? Must we live in isolation of all others in the world to preserve our mutual beliefs? If not, is community more than coming together for an hour on Sunday morning, singing the same songs, and bowing in corporate prayer?

BIBLICAL COMMUNITY IN THE EARLY CHURCH

In Acts 2, the birth of the church came in a mighty way, with fire and passion after a unified seeking of God's presence, an event so powerful thousands were added to their number in a single day. The church continued to grow as believers

> Devoted themselves to the apostles' teaching and to fellowship, to the breaking of bread and to prayer.
> (v. 42 NIV)

An amazing thing happened. As Christians bonded together, the world tasted the saltiness of their joy, love, and peace. Not because they sold everything and lived together. The magnet was in their love for one another. No one was greater than anyone else, and together they met each other's needs. They prayed together and cared for one another.

Some might say communal living was a first century phenomenon in church development. I wonder, has the body of Christ doused our influence in exchange for rugged individualism and prideful promotion of our isms, programs, and ministries? Have we pursued uniqueness rather than unity? Is this part of the reason the world hates us and wants nothing to do with church people?

How do we get back to God's original plan for fellowship of those hearts united in love for him?

BIBLICAL COMMUNITY AS GOD INTENDS

As we grow in purpose, wisdom, and understanding, as we become holier — become more like the Father— we want to demonstrate this new heart and new mind in all our relationships. When we focus on whose we are, our individual egos melt, molding with our fellow believers into a new element, a community rich in flavor, a commodity to be desired.

> So we, being many, are one body in Christ, and individually members of one another. (Romans 12:5)

A popular Christmas carol invites all to "Deck the halls with boughs of holly." As I sing the carol, I am struck with the simplicity of the call to come together in fellowship: "Sing we joyous, all together ... heedless of the wind and weather."

Something about Christmas brings out the socialite in the most reclusive. There is a sense the season is to be shared. But what about the rest of the year? When the New Year is old, and the fervor of the season has waned? Will the desire for fellowship burn out with the return to the mundane? Is the art of fellowship dead in the church? Maybe the vinegar of the world has eroded our concept of true fellowship.

Over the centuries, the church in America became a social institution, exclusive clubs where only those who looked, dressed, and acted a certain way felt welcomed. Perhaps Christians cloistered themselves out of fear of contamination. Losing its ability to salve a hurting world, is there any wonder church attendance has fallen dramatically over the last several decades?

Fortunately, many churches today are experiencing a resurgence of a social Christianity and have come out from the vestibule to the streets of the needy. Believers are spending less time organizing the monthly potluck dinner and are more engaged in community work. Volunteers stack cans in food pantries, and women's groups knit blankets for premature babies.

A Different Kind of Aloofness

I wonder if the impact on those outside of the church might still be perceived as a different kind of aloofness. Do we inadvertently demean in our effort to uplift? For all our good deeds fall short, if we are not motivated to reach outside our walls with the same love found within. If we extend our fellowship with only a handout and not a handshake, have we given the same subliminal message as our secluded forebears? Does fellowship require more than erecting a homeless shelter? Have we traded one form of indifference for another more insidious, one that hides beneath a veil of caring? Or does God require us to extend his grace through genuine affection for even those who do not think as we do or value what we value?

True Fellowship

Fellowship denotes a sense of belonging.

Our fellowship with others is an extension of our fellowship with God. He loved us even in our iniquities. When we stop warring with him and accept his provision of salvation, our spirits begin to align with his. Our joy is being made complete. Perhaps not practiced every day, perhaps in stages of development. Nonetheless, the spiritual work has begun and will continue—ours to claim.

When we relate to others with this same unconditional love extended to us, then—and only then—can we begin to appreciate the true spirit of fellowship—whether inside the church walls, lunch with a friend, or ministering to the homeless. For our fellowship mirrors the joy we find in God's grace. This then is our joyous measure:

> But if we walk in the light, as He is in the light, we have fellowship with one another. (1 John 1:7)

The Greek word *eklesis* is sometimes translated as church. But the word actually means "assembly." The Greek word more accurately translated as "church" is *kuriake*—literally, "belonging to the Lord."

In modern times, church has become synonymous with a gathering place. When we say, "I went to church," we are saying we went to a place where people were gathered together in like mind. Sometimes this is a building. Sometimes this can be outdoors as is the case with many third-world Christian communities. The coming together might be in the open or in secret. The common thread is that worshipers are bonded together in a shared worship experience.

When Christians come together or assemble for a singular purpose, rather than a commitment to an organization or a building, the Spirit is able to move in ways the human mind cannot fathom. This is what God desires for his salt.

A COMMUNITY OF SALT

What then does a community of salt look like?
Acts 1 gives us some idea.

1. They were together.
2. They were with one accord.
3. They continued in prayer.

Unity and prayer were the prelude to Pentecost. The same does happen today when we wait before God in desperate, believing, fervent, and unhurried prayer. In those times, we are visited with the energizing power of the Spirit of God. Prayer brings congregations together and builds a sense of harmony, peace, and love. God's desire for his children.

One long-time member wants to enjoy the hymns of yore. "'The Old Rugged Cross' still gives me a thrill," he says. A younger adult feels she is the most blessed when the worship team bangs out a rousing rendition of "Fear Not." Two vastly differing music styles with equal potential to edify the body of Christ.

One board leader believes Communion should be provided at every corporate worship event. The board is inundated with carefully selected Scripture verses for support of his opinion. In contrast, the board vice-chair believes Communion, an important element of worship, is more than the passing of bread and consumption of a wine substitute. Consequently, he believes Communion should be expressed in other ways during worship.

Divisiveness is the devil's area of expertise. When the need to fulfill an individual definition of what constitutes worship replaces the willingness to submit to the good of the body, Satan adds the heat allowing the yeast of discontent to rise. "Showers of Blessings" cease to fall, services dry up, and hungry believers seek nourishment elsewhere.

In this world of diverse spiritual backgrounds and conflicting generational expectations, how does the church of today develop a worship experience that will dispel disparity and bring about unity? How does God want his salt to worship together?

The question is as old as humankind. The first argument over worship styles occurred between Cain and Abel with fatal results.

Paul understood how the spirit of disparity would intrude upon corporate worship when its members allowed the need for self-expression to exceed the good of the body.

By lifting up a unified testament to God's amazing grace, Satan would have to flee. He cannot remain where there is harmony of purpose—our purpose being giving thanks to the God of the Ages and to his son, Jesus Christ. What greater source of unity can there be?

When King Hezekiah reinstated temple worship, he divided the priests and Levites according to certain duties. Some were to offer sacrifices, others would provide the thanksgivings, others would minister, and still others would sing praises (2 Chronicles 3:1). Each participant was given a specific function. Hezekiah instructed the worshippers to provide for the priests so they in turn could devote themselves to the Law of the Lord. The people gave so generously, the temple burst at the seams requiring storehouses to be built. Their giving did not come by way of a King's command but from hearts yearning to worship.

After Pentecost, we are told the believers were energized with harmony.

> And they continued steadfastly in the apostles' doctrine and fellowship, in the breaking of bread, and in prayers. (Acts 2:42)

They came together with a hungering for God; their only purpose to worship. The how was inconsequential. Everyone was blessed because each entered the experience with joy and anticipation of blessings. Perhaps this is why Paul reminded his son-in-the-faith, Timothy, of the importance of unity:

> Therefore I exhort first of all that supplications, prayers, intercessions, and giving of thanks be made for all men, for kings and all who are in authority, that we may lead a quiet and peaceable life in all godliness and reverence. For this is good and acceptable in the sight of God our Savior, who desires all men to be saved and

to come to the knowledge of the truth. For there is one God and one Mediator between God and men, the Man Christ Jesus, who gave Himself a ransom for all, to be testified in due time. (1 Timothy 2:1–6)

Judaic Influence

The concept of coming together for worship was not new to Jewish converts to Christianity. The Temple, or synagogue, was the central point of most Jewish communities. The concept of our spiritual relationships as being a familial relationship most likely developed from this origin.

In Old Testament times, Jews understood through the law the importance of responsibility and commitment to one another. They were bonded by a common heritage, not merely by blood. To be members of the same people meant that each person was responsible for the welfare of all others.

As the New Testament church developed, much of the Old Testament model remained. They were truly one body and community. Necessity brought them together as well as a bond of like-mindedness.

While we enjoy friendships with many Christians—go out to dinner or have fellowships in our homes—the sense of communal bonding sometimes seems missing from our collective worship experience of today.

In any church we've attended, getting to know people beyond facial and name recognition has proven to be a challenge. Not because people are self-centered or don't care. More often than not, the busyness of our lives tends to create a disconnect. Perhaps our culture has not produced the need to bond in the same intimacy as the early church. Yet, God's call to his salt is to bond together in peace, in harmony.

The church today is no less willing to come to the aid of someone who is hurting. The pity is the church has become so fragmented needs are more difficult to identify unless someone speaks up.

We are often not aware because we are not bonded as the church once was. Perhaps our fragmented churches is one way we've allowed the world's vinegar to seep into the salt of our Christian relationships.

Most Christians today make limited commitments to other Christians. They can be counted on for a number of carefully specified activities. The remaining parts of their lives are private. Our commitments as Christians are usually no different from our other commitments, such as our jobs.

While many Christians remain committed to their biological families, many do not feel the need to commit to their Christian community or church fellowship in the same way. Many believe they are already over-committed, especially young families with very active children. They feel as though they have little left to give to the church, though many do, amazingly so.

Fellowship in the New Testament used another Greek word: *koinonia*, commonly translated as "fellowship." Unfortunately, in our English context, we interpret this as a loosely connected group.

Often times, a family may leave a congregation with the complaint, "There's a lack of fellowship."

The pastor scratches his head. "How can this be? Just look at our calendar of events?"

Christians still seek the bond once prevalent in the early church. A connectedness through purpose, belief, and love for one another. A community of like-minded hopes, vision, and purpose.

THE HUMAN QUEST FOR COMMUNITY

The word has become very common in today's culture: "African American community," "LBGTQ community," "Latino community," and the list goes on. Unfortunately, this categorization in the world has divided cultures rather than unified different groups. Nonetheless, the trend demonstrates the human desire to find a community of love, understanding, and acceptance.

Said the introductory song of the once popular sitcom, *Cheers*, "you want to be where everybody knows your name."

Why then do parishioners not sense this bond? What is lacking?

Perhaps today's churches have forgotten the primary unity of the New Testament church. The Holy Spirit, the provision for the understanding, love, and acceptance that human beings seek.

> The grace of the Lord Jesus Christ, and the love of God, and the communion of the Holy Spirit be with you all. Amen. (2 Corinthians 13:14)

Today's culture does not lend toward the concept of shared possessions in the tangible sense. Yet the Holy Spirit provides a willingness to share our possession when a need is identified—in essence, a much deeper sharing than potluck suppers. In true Christian fellowship, we do not live for ourselves alone. We are continually mindful of our community members in thought, deed, and prayer.

COMMITMENTPHOBIA

According to many psychiatrists, there is an alarming growth in the occurrence of a social disorder called "commitmentphobia" or fear of commitment. The disorder is manifested, not only in basic human relationships, but in the workplace as well. Unable to engage in the purposes of their companies, commitmentphobes become quickly bored with their jobs. They either quit, are fired, or their employers impose fewer expectations with the result of lost productivity.

Commitmentphobia impacts the sufferer on the most primitive levels. Yet, the commitmentphobe is difficult to spot until after the harm is done. The commitmentphobe will often talk the talk but cannot walk the walk. While on the surface the commitmentphobe hints at a future, the relationship soon crumbles because the commitmentphobe cannot give the personal investment to the relationship. Furthermore, if an individual cannot commit to another human being, how then can there be commitment to a cause or a group?

Why do people fear commitment? Psychologists believe commitmentphobia is rooted in a fear of the unknown or a pervasive need to control. Deeper roots may be found in an early traumatic event such as, particularly in the church experience, a disappointment in a trusted authority figure through abuse or neglect.

But for most of us, the failure to commit may be as simple as lacking the compelling emotional criteria uniting us to something larger than ourselves.

Regardless of its roots, commitmentphobia may be one of the most pervasive issues within the church. No wonder non-believers shy away from attending churches where its members are unable to team together for the common cause of Christ. Such disharmony most often is the result of spiritual commitmentphobia—the inability to engage beyond what pleases or is convenient for the individual.

How many times have we heard someone say they left a church because "I wasn't being fed"?

"If there's nothing in it for me, I'm not interested" is the world's viewpoint.

Commitment, like love, does not seek its own reward. It does not flaunt itself or boast. It flows out of our desire to please rather than get, propelling the believer to action rather than fear.

Only through the power of the Holy Spirit can God's salt be a true community.

FOR FURTHER STUDY OR GROUP DISCUSSION

1. Read Psalm 16:8.

> I have set the LORD always before me;
> Because He is at my right hand I shall not be moved.

- Is our personal faith separate from corporate faith? Why or why not?

- How does a corporate experience help our faith grow?

2. Read Romans 11.15 and compare to 1 Kings 19:1–18.

Sometimes, such as in the workplace or at social events, we feel as though we are the only "righteous" people around. Paul says there is a _____ according to the election of _____.

Elijah flees for his life. In the previous chapter, he has just had the mountaintop experience of bringing rain, resulting in putting to death over 400 prophets of Baal, and Jezebel sought vengeance. Now he feels alone and wants to die.

> So he said, "I have been very zealous for the LORD God of hosts; for the children of Israel have forsaken Your covenant, torn down Your altars, and killed Your prophets with the sword. I alone am left; and they seek to take my life. (1 Kings 19:10)

God sent an angel to minister to him. Then after wandering for forty days and nights, God sent him back to work. His mission was not yet complete. He reminded Elijah that he had reserved a remnant in Israel. Elijah was not alone.

> Yet I have reserved seven thousand in Israel, all whose knees have not bowed to Baal, and every mouth that has not kissed him. (1 Kings 19:18)

- Has there been a time in your life you have felt all alone in your cause for Christ? How did God meet that sense of loneliness?

3. Read Psalm 133:1.

> Behold, how good and how pleasant it is
> For brethren to dwell together in unity!

- How is being part of a community of believers a blessing?

4. Read Ephesians 2:19–22.

> Now, therefore, you are no longer strangers and foreigners, but fellow citizens with the saints and members of the household of God, having been built on the foundation of the apostles and prophets, Jesus Christ Himself being the chief cornerstone, in whom the whole building, being fitted together, grows into a holy temple in the Lord, in whom you also are being built together for a dwelling place of God in the Spirit.

- Instead of strangers we are _____. How does that impact the way we might worship?
- What is the foundation this fellowship is built upon?

- Who is the cornerstone for this household of God? How does this cause unity within the body of believers?

- How are believers joined together to build the dwelling place of God?

5. Read Ephesians 4:29–31.

   Let no corrupt word proceed out of your mouth, but what is good for necessary edification, that it may impart grace to the hearers. And do not grieve the Holy Spirit of God, by whom you were sealed for the day of redemption. Let all bitterness, wrath, anger, clamor, and evil speaking be put away from you, with all malice.

   - According to Paul, how should we conduct our corporate speech?

   - What attitudes grieve the Holy Spirit in the body of believers?

   - Paul says to put away all malice. How do we do that?

6. Read James 4:1–2.

   Where do wars and fights come from among you? Do they not come from your desires for pleasure that war in your members? You lust and do not have. You murder and covet and cannot obtain. You fight and[j] war. Yet you do not have because you do not ask.

- Where does James say disagreements within the body originate?

- Why do our corporate prayers seem ineffectual?

7. Read James 5:13–16.

    Is anyone among you suffering? Let him pray. Is anyone cheerful? Let him sing psalms. Is anyone among you sick? Let him call for the elders of the church, and let them pray over him, anointing him with oil in the name of the Lord. And the prayer of faith will save the sick, and the Lord will raise him up. And if he has committed sins, he will be forgiven. Confess your trespasses to one another, and pray for one another, that you may be healed. The effective, fervent prayer of a righteous man avails much.

    - What components of community worship does James suggest?

    - Have you experienced a time when you needed prayer support from other believers?

    - Why do you think we hesitate to ask for prayer?

- Note James's instruction to forgive, confess, and pray for one another. Does unconfessed sin and an unforgiving spirit interfere with effective prayer for one another?

- Sometimes we may be suffering. Sometimes we may be cheerful. One day we need prayer support and another we can eagerly pray for others.

8. Read Philippians 2:1–2.

> Therefore if there is any encouragement and comfort in Christ [as there certainly is in abundance], if there is any consolation of love, if there is any fellowship [that we share] in the Spirit, if [there is] any [great depth of] affection and compassion, make my joy complete by being of the same mind, having the same love [toward one another], knit together in spirit, intent on one purpose [and living a life that reflects your faith and spreads the gospel—the good news regarding salvation through faith in Christ]. (AMP)

- How do our lives reflect our faith in our relationships with other believers?

- Who is Paul referring to when he says we should be of the same mind?

- How do we demonstrate the same love Christ has for us in our relationships with other believers?

9. Read Colossians 3:12–17.

> Therefore, as the elect of God, holy and beloved, put on tender mercies, kindness, humility, meekness, longsuffering; bearing with one another, and forgiving one another, if anyone has a complaint against another; even as Christ forgave you, so you also must do. But above all these things put on love, which is the bond of perfection. And let the peace of God rule in your hearts, to which also you were called in one body; and be thankful. Let the word of Christ dwell in you richly in all wisdom, teaching and admonishing one another in psalms and hymns and spiritual songs, singing with grace in your hearts to the Lord. And whatever you do in word or deed, do all in the name of the Lord Jesus, giving thanks to God the Father through Him.

- How does God describe the "elect of God?" _____ and _____.

- What attributes does Paul desire believers to "put on" _____, _____, _____, _____, and _____.

- If we possess the above attributes, bearing one another and forgiving one another will be realized as a natural outgrowth from this fruit of the Spirit.

- To what are we called?

- What should we do in the name of the Lord Jesus?

10. Read Romans 16:16, 1 Corinthians 16:20, 2 Corinthians 13:12, 1 Thessalonians 5:26.

- What instruction do these verses contain?

- Why is this an important aspect of the community of believers?

Some scholars point out that the concept of "holy kiss" is deeper than a mere physical contact. The kiss was customary in Biblical times as a form of greeting, especially among close relationships such as family or friends. Sometimes, as in the kiss of Judas, the gesture could be insincere or deceitful. Paul distinguishes the holy kiss as one in which even gentiles and Jews could embrace one another. In other words, set aside their differences for the sake of joined worship. The act of a holy kiss signified acceptance.

- Given our germophobic culture and suspicion of close contact, how might we demonstrate a "holy kiss" in our current cultural climate?

Chapter Six—Called to be Holy

When I worked for a smoking cessation program, I counseled smokers desiring to quit the habit. The most important truth to grasp was true and lasting change only came from within. First one needed to identify why they should quit. Lasting changed behavior can only be achieved as a result of a changed attitude.

THE TANGENCY OF FAITH AND WORKS

C.S. Lewis in *Mere Christianity* demonstrates how faith and works are in tangent. Because we believe, our outward person is changed. The things we valued no longer hold appeal.

Paul understood how the outward man changed with an inward striving to be different:

> Yet indeed I also count all things loss for the excellence of the knowledge of Christ Jesus my Lord, for whom I have suffered the loss of all things, and count them as rubbish, that I may gain Christ. (Philippians 3:8)

And again, later in the chapter:

> Brethren, I do not count myself to have apprehended; but one thing I do, forgetting those things which are behind and reaching forward to those things which are ahead, I press toward the goal for the prize of the upward call of God in Christ Jesus. (Philippians 3:13–14)

Forgetting what is behind can prove difficult. Not just our failures. Whenever I took pride in a good accomplishment, my mother would remind me, "Don't rest on your laurels."

In other words, "That's good. Now keep on doing good." We get so bogged down in our failures (feeling defeated) or successes (pride in what we've already accomplished) we don't move forward.

A changed heart will ultimately change our attitudes. As our attitudes change, our behavior and values change.

God has called his salt to behave differently than the vinegar of the world.

SHOULD VS. WANT

In an earlier chapter we explored how God is transforming us into his image. The old adage says, "It is easy to have a green lawn in May. But only a dedicated gardener has one in August."

I can relate. Gardening is not one of my strong points, having neither the talent nor inclination toward the task. I think I should work on trimming my lawn, but I seem to find other priorities.

I know the drill. I hear it from my doctor with every visit. Lose weight, eat more nutritiously, and get more exercise. After my physician has kindly reminded me of the benefits derived from healthier life-style choices, I make well-intentioned promises of changed behaviors.

I pride myself on those good intentions.

Sadly, however, my behaviors slowly drift back to my comfortable, unhealthy choices within a few weeks. "I just don't have enough will power," I tell myself. "Why can't I do better?"

The problem in compliance is not from a lack of knowledge but rather from a lack of true want. Oh, it would be nice to be as beautiful as Miss America, as athletic as an Olympic champion, and as enthusiastic as a political candidate. But do I have a sufficient want for these things? Am I willing to make the sacrifices and commit to the long haul to gain my desire?

Attitudes regarding change are shaped according to whether we desire the change out of a feeling of guilt or whether the change is motivated due to a conviction. The shoulds are a result of guilt—the wants are born from conviction.

Guilt is laden with self-incrimination and self-loathing—a heavy burden to carry. Guilt tends to slow progress and cause depression. Guilt may propel us into action initially, but the momentum is difficult to sustain. When we fail, we convince ourselves there is some intrinsic flaw dooming us to a cycle of attempts and failures. With each failure, the desire to try again is diminished.

When we truly want to change, we are convicted toward change. Conviction alters our perspective, renews our energies, and drives us toward a positive outcome. Even if a first attempt is unsuccessful, we will keep trying until we experience ultimate success.

What of our spiritual lifestyles? We believe we should read the Bible more, attend church regularly, and give a tithe to the Lord. Every devotional article we read reminds us of the benefits when we do these things. Yet our striving toward these goals abates as life's mundane needs erode our best intentions.

God does not desire us to follow a blind pattern of religiosity. This is vinegar. Doing good deeds, merely because one should do them, will produce meaningless exercise that does little to uplift the believer. Even the world suggests one should be kind, helpful, and generous—admirable qualities.

Then what is the solution? We know we should be different. How do we transcend guilt to conviction to ultimate change?

God provides his salt with the Holy Spirit. The fruit of this gift accomplishes what our meager efforts cannot.

In Part II, we'll explore the meaning of living faith through the power of the Spirit, or God's recipe for victorious Christian Living.

For now, let us focus on the fact God has called salt to live differently than the world. This difference is the result of a new heart, a new mind, a sense of purpose, the development of wisdom and understanding in the believer's life—the outward evidence of inward transformation.

God places a hunger within the believer that propels us toward God's word. Rather than condemn our past, he uses our failure as a lamp to show us what our future could be when we walk in obedience. As we grow in our desire to walk more closely with God, we no longer pray simply because that's what a Christian should do. We pray because our day is incomplete without spending time alone with him.

Perhaps this pursuit of the shoulds is the reason we act no different than the vinegar of the world, those who strive because they believe being good is admirable. Perhaps why our lives become flavorless, and those around us can see no value in being a Christian. If striving in our own efforts out of duty could have brought our salvation, could have truly changed our heart, we would have no need of a Savior.

THE QUEST FOR DISCIPLINE

Paul talks often about discipline in his life. Like an athlete who trains his body for the event in which he is competing, discipline is a life-long process.

We want instant change.

We forget a lot of falling down happens before we stand up tall.

When my grandson learned to walk, he gradually stood away from the piece of furniture that supported him. Then he took a few steps forward, teetering somewhat. When he fell, he crawled back to where he took his first step, renewed his confidence, and ventured out again. This is how we grow and change. When we fall, we must return to the cross—the place of our identity, the place where we took our first faith step.

Effective self-discipline boils down to motivation. Dedication also means to give special attention to focus, expand effort, and loyalty. In a previous chapter we talked a great deal about commitment to a community. The same applies to commitment to change. Our level of commitment will be proportionate to our level of motivation.

Even the world understands this truth. In order to change, one needs a different mindset. The world, however, views change from an ego-centric point of view. If I want a raise at work, I need to perform my tasks in such a way to show my worth. If I want to be attractive, I must dress a certain way. The more we want something, the more willing we become to sacrifice our normal living to gain the desired outcome.

Rather than follow the world's advice, Paul urges us to adopt the mind of Christ.

> Let this mind be in you which was also in Christ Jesus, who, being in the form of God, did not consider it robbery to be equal with God, but made Himself of no reputation, taking the form of a bondservant, and coming in the likeness of men. And being found in appearance as a man, He humbled Himself and became obedient to the point of death, even the death of the cross. (Philippians 2:5–8)

The difference between salt and vinegar is the root of our desire to be holy.

Satan tricks us by putting our own egos in front of our desire to please God. We become frustrated and believe we are ineffective because we think the change comes from what we do, not from who and whose we are.

> There are many plans in a man's heart,
> Nevertheless the LORD's counsel—that will stand.
> (Proverbs 19:21)

If we fail, we can cry out to God.-We can tell him our frustrations. We are his child and can come to his mercy seat when we hurt or we are angry. We can crawl back to the place where God first got hold of us—the place where our love for God began. This is the most important aspect of gaining discipline, the willingness to return to the place of our first encounter with Grace.

LEARNING TO WALK

Just as parents delight in each new advance their child makes, God delights in us as we learn to walk in his ways, the reason he has called us to be his salt. He claps and rejoices with each step we take.

> My brethren, count it all joy when you fall into various trials, knowing that the testing of your faith produces patience. But let patience have its perfect work, that you may be perfect and complete, lacking nothing. (James 1:2–4)

We get in God's way of our metamorphosis because we doubt he wants us as we are. We cannot accept ourselves as the creatures he has created us to be. We feel we should change in order to win God's approval. So we try in our own efforts.

This leads to disappointment. We feel we have failed the Lord. We even doubt our Christianity. We doubt our calling or our purpose. When we focus on our limitations and our human abilities, we will only see our lack, not the raw material God uses to mold us into what he wants us to be.

The world's wisdom says if we want to be different than what we are, we should model after the kind of person we want to be. The world says if you want to be thin, you need to think like a thin person. If you want to be wealthy, you must think like the person who acquires wealth. If you desire power, you must model yourself after the powerful and be like they are.

The problem is our behavior will ultimately betray our true heart and mind.

For example, money is not the problem. The love of money is. We will seek after what we love (1 Timothy 6:10). And when we love money, we will be corrupted by greed. We will shape our lives according to what we desire.

Why Paul advises:

> Finally, brethren, whatever things are true, whatever things are noble, whatever things are just, whatever things are pure, whatever things are lovely, whatever things are of good report, if there is any virtue and if there is anything praiseworthy—meditate on these things. The things which you learned and received and heard and saw in me, these do, and the God of peace will be with you. (Philippians 4:8–9)

Unfortunately, our current Christian climate has placed a high value on the acquisition of things. Yes, God has blessed some individuals with wealth, so they can bless others. But we set our eyes and our hearts upon the external, the vinegar of the world. And when we don't have what we think we deserve, we become discouraged. Christians are not immune from this world view of wanting and striving for what we desire.

If we are feeling discouraged, perhaps feeling God is far away and no longer active in our corporeal lives, we can return to the cross—our home base for everything in our spiritual realm.

Here we can ask him to show us any unconfessed sin blocking our ability to move forward in our Christian walk.

> And see if there is any wicked way in me,
> And lead me in the way everlasting. (Psalm 139:24)

Asa had a great start to his reign, but he became prideful—deceived to believe his successes came from his own cleverness. Sometimes, like King Asa, we look to the world's wisdom rather than take our concerns to the Lord (2 Chronicles 16).

Is God to Blame?

We want immediate results to our prayers and for our circumstances to change instantly. The world is quick to point a finger and look for blame. Even Martha, a close friend to Jesus, blamed him for her brother's death (John 11). "If you had been here," she said, "my brother would not have died." (paraphrased) She could not understand why Jesus had not come more quickly. He'd been told he was needed, yet he delayed. She failed to understand, Lazarus's death was not punishment nor a failure of friendship. This circumstance had come to demonstrate Jesus's authority over death.

How often we play "if only." We think if the circumstance had been different, the outcome would have been more favorable. We even blame our failures on God's slow response to our dilemma. We forget God is in charge, and he will utilize our seeming failures as much as our successes to bring about his master plan to change his salt into his representation—to be holy as he is holy.

God has always desired for his salt to walk in righteousness and continues to call his salt to walk in holiness.

> Let us hear the conclusion of the whole matter;
>   Fear God and keep His commandments,
>   For this is man's all. (Ecclesiastes 12:13)

Think on These Things

Scripture provides a litany of those things we should pursue, the outward expression of a heart that is one with God:

> Finally, believers, whatever is true, whatever is honorable and worthy of respect, whatever is right and confirmed by God's word, whatever is pure and wholesome, whatever is lovely and brings peace, whatever is admirable and of good repute; if there is any excellence, if there is anything worthy of praise,

think continually on these things [center your mind on them, and implant them in your heart].The things which you have learned and received and heard and seen in me, practice these things [in daily life], and the God [who is the source] of peace and well-being will be with you. (Philippians 4:8–9 AMP)

In the above reference, Paul gives us guidelines for a positive thought life.

- Things that are true

But where do we find truth? God's word. God desires the believer to weigh their actions, their day to day pursuits against his Word. Sometimes believers tend to examine the truth of the world—brittle truth that changes according to the latest philosophy. God's word is a permanent backdrop for our decision making.

- Things that are honorable

When evaluating or calculating a decision, God desires our choices will honor him first. The world has its own definition of honor, a code devised by man. God has provided us with the example of his Son, why Paul exhorts the early church to follow Christ's example in thought and deed.

- Things worthy of respect

Our "in your face" world, often admires the feisty and assertive soul. The one who never backs down though sometimes in the wrong. The problem is not with feeling we are right. The problem emanates from a feeling our rights mean more than someone else's. Most disrespect comes from an immediate reaction to self-interest. "Get out of my way. I'm coming through." We deem our needs, wants, and desires are more important than anyone else's. We are happy to love our neighbor as long as we are not inconvenienced.

- Things that have a good report

People are always watching. Some take great pleasure in finding a weakness and exploiting that weakness for their own benefit. We have become a culture of blame, as well as lovers of gossip. We enjoy hearing the latest bits of juicy dirt on celebrities and sharing what we've just learned on social media or the office breakroom. God desires for his salt to take the road of positivity. Our words should be edged by what demonstrates God's goodness and love.

- Things that are virtuous

Salt will choose those things that honor God and demonstrate our love for one another—even those persons who use us in hurtful ways or those whose value systems are opposite ours. We can only truly choose good over evil through the power of the Holy Spirit.

- Things that are praiseworthy

When my son would rebel against his teachers whom he thought were unfair or unjust, I told him, "Argue from a point of right. Then, and only then, will your argument be credible. If you do wrong because another person has done wrong, what praise is in those deeds?"

- Think on these continually

Scripture says to think on these things continually because the Holy Spirit's guidance protects us from the negativity of the world.

FOR FURTHER STUDY OR GROUP DISCUSSION

1. Read 1 Peter 1:13–16.

    Therefore gird up the loins of your mind, be sober, and rest your hope fully upon the grace that is to be brought to you at the revelation of Jesus Christ; as obedient children, not conforming yourselves to the former lusts, as in your ignorance; but as He who called you is holy, you also be holy in all your conduct, because it is written, "Be holy, for I am holy."

- Why does God command us to be holy?

- What does "gird of the loins of your mind" mean?

- How do we accomplish this?

- How do we reconcile our imperfect humanity with God's holiness?

2. Read Psalm 127:1.

Unless the LORD builds the house,
They labor in vain who build it;
Unless the LORD guards the city.
The watchman stays awake in vain.

- How does this verse apply to our spiritual house and city?

- God knows our vulnerabilities and protects us as we seek to serve him. Of course, we are vulnerable to physical injury. But even then, God is in control. How does thought life impact our ability to imitate God's holiness?

3. Read Ephesians 4:26–32.

Be angry, and do not sin: do not let the sun go down on your wrath, nor give place to the devil. Let him who stole steal no longer, but rather let him labor, working with his hands what is good, that he may have something to give him who has need. Let no corrupt word proceed out of your mouth, but what is good for necessary edification, that it may impart grace to the hearers. And do not grieve the Holy Spirit of God, by whom you were sealed for the day of redemption. Let all bitterness, wrath, anger, clamor, and evil speaking be put away from you, with all malice. And be kind to one another, tenderhearted, forgiving one another, even as God in Christ forgave you.

- We examined these verses in a previous chapter as these words relate to the community of believers. How do these verses now relate to a pursuit of holiness?

- How might these responses to circumstances or attitudes toward others "give place to the devil"?

- What Godly alternative responses to difficult or charged situations does Paul desire God's salt to emulate?

4. Read Proverbs 18: 6–8, 21.

A fool's lips enter into contention,
And his mouth calls for blows.
A fool's mouth is his destruction,
And his lips are the snare of his soul.
The words of a talebearer are like tasty trifles,

And they go down into the inmost body.
Death and life are in the power of the tongue,
And those who love it will eat its fruit.

- In what ways can the tongue, or our speech, be an instrument for Satan's destructive influence or a reflection of God's holiness?

- How does this hold true in our written communication as well? Is your testimony in your tweet?

5. Read Proverbs 18:14.

   The spirit of a man will sustain him in sickness,
   But who can bear a broken spirit?

   - How does a wounded spirit keep us from demonstrating God's holiness in our relationships?

   - How does a Godly spirit sustain us in times of trouble or sickness?

6. Read Psalm 141:3–4.

   Set a guard, O LORD, over my mouth;
   Keep watch over the door of my lips.

Do not incline my heart to any evil thing,
To practice wicked works
With men who work iniquity;
And do not let me eat of their delicacies.

- What guard does the Holy Spirit provide to keep our speech pure?

- Are you considering confrontation with someone?

- Ask yourself: Is what I say true? Is what I say loving? Why am I saying these words? Do these words reflect the character of God?

7. Read Luke 22:47–51.

   And while He was still speaking, behold, a multitude; and he who was called Judas, one of the twelve, went before them and drew near to Jesus to kiss Him. But Jesus said to him, "Judas, are you betraying the Son of Man with a kiss?"

   When those around Him saw what was going to happen, they said to Him, "Lord, shall we strike with the sword?" And one of them struck the servant of the high priest and cut off his right ear. But Jesus answered and said, "Permit even this." And He touched his ear and healed him.

   - Why do you think Jesus allowed Judas to betray him?

- What did Jesus mean when he told the disciple who cut off the servant's ear, "Permit even this."?

- The world sees this meekness of Jesus as weakness. How was Jesus's example in the garden a Godly example of how his salt should live?

- How have some Christians allowed the wisdom of the world to corrupt their Godly example? (For example, the use of Social Media)

8. Read 1 Corinthians 10:13.

   No temptation has overtaken you except such as is common to man; but God is faithful, who will not allow you to be tempted beyond what you are able, but with the temptation will also make the way of escape, that you may be able to bear it.

   - Does this verse apply to the temptation to follow the world's wisdom when such wisdom is opposite God's wisdom?

   - Have you ever experienced a time when the Lord helped you overcome a temptation to react in an ungodly manner to a given circumstance?

9. Read James 3:16–17.

   For where envy and self-seeking exist, confusion and every evil thing are there. But the wisdom that is from above is first pure, then peaceable, gentle, willing to yield, full of mercy and good fruits, without partiality and without hypocrisy.

   - How does Paul describe the wisdom "from above"?

   - How does this contrast with the world's wisdom?

10. Read 2 Peter 1: 5–8.

    But also for this very reason, giving all diligence, add to your faith virtue, to virtue knowledge, to knowledge self-control, to self-control perseverance, to perseverance godliness, to godliness brotherly kindness, and to brotherly kindness love. For if these things are yours and abound, you will be neither barren nor unfruitful in the knowledge of our Lord Jesus Christ.

    - How do we add these things to our faith? Do we obtain these attributes through our own efforts?

    - What is the result of obtaining the fruit listed above?

    - How are these attributes intertwined? What do these attributes evidence?

Part II

God's Recipe for Victorious Living

Believing is Easy

Believing is easy
Even devils believe
Faith is the difficult choice
The wind howls
Belief scatters like dandelion seeds
Against the rocks of disillusionment
Faith indestructible
Rebuilds
Faith chooses hope
Declines despair
The stirred soul
Like the river's peaceful flow
Restored after the storm

Poem by Linda Wood Rondeau

Chapter Seven—Salt Transcends

"I believe in Christianity
as I believe that the sun has risen:
not only because I see it,
but because by it I see everything else."
— C.S. Lewis

"Little victories," my mother would say each time she circumvented a natural tendency to lash out or give in to a temptation.

God intends for his salt to live victoriously. This was his plan from the beginning of time. Faith that transcends the pull of the world and its vinegar of wisdom.

PAUL'S SIMPLE GOSPEL MESSAGE

Paul is honest about his human frailty. He mentions his weakness, his thorn in the flesh that made him weak. Often God does not take away our weakness, rather he desires for his salt to rise above the weakness.

> And I, brethren, when I came to you, did not come with excellence of speech or of wisdom declaring to you the testimony of God. For I determined not to know anything among you except Jesus Christ and Him crucified. I was with you in weakness, in fear, and in much trembling. And my speech and my preaching were not with persuasive words of human wisdom, but in demonstration of the Spirit and of power, that your faith should not be in the wisdom of men but in the power of God. (1 Corinthians 2:1–5)

Though Paul was among the most educated of Pharisees in his time, he chose to teach the simple truth of the gospel. Christ saves. The reason for his simplicity? So our faith would not rest on humankind's wisdom, the vinegar of this world, but rather our faith would transform us into God's precious salt. Not merely transform but also sustain and transcend.

THE SPIRIT OF VICTORY

We discussed in a previous chapter—the Spirit brings us into truth in order to comprehend the deep things of God. And this truth is the power by which we live victoriously—a faith that transcends any obstacle the enemy puts in our way.

By the Spirit's power we can rejoice in troubling circumstances.

> Rejoice in the Lord always. Again I will say, rejoice! (Philippians 4:4)

When we rejoice, worry over our difficulties diminishes. Failure, fear, anger, frustration, disappointment fade in the light of God's awesome power.

Our faith walk is often a good news/bad news journey. There are times when we experience earthly joy and pleasures as well as abundant blessings. Sometimes, those blessings are hidden in the trial. The old adage "Every cloud has a silver lining" has spiritual truth as well.

Peter was elated when he finally understood who Jesus was. "You are the Christ." I imagine he fairly danced, every fiber of his being filled with joy. But when Jesus was arrested, this same Peter's faith faltered. How could this possibly happen to the Messiah?

We know from Scripture Peter denied the Lord three times (John 21:15–17). And once Peter's faith was restored, Jesus gave him back this joy through allowing him to repeat his affirmation three times as he asked the question, "Do you love me?" Peter answered, "Yes, Lord, I love you." (paraphrased) His joy helped him transcend his grief.

PREPARED FOR VICTORY

Throughout Christ's journey with his disciples, he prepared them for what was to come—though they would comprehend his words in retrospect rather than at the time of the telling.

> And when they had sung a hymn, they went out to the Mount of Olives. Then Jesus said to them, "All of you will be made to stumble because of Me this night, for it is written:
> 'I will strike the Shepherd,
> And the sheep will be scattered.'
> But after I have been raised, I will go before you to Galilee. (Mark 14:26–28 NIV)

Good news/bad news. Perhaps tradition had forgotten the prophecy foretold in the Old Testament concerning the Messiah.

> "Awake, O sword, against My Shepherd,
> Against the Man who is My Companion,"
> Says the LORD of hosts.
> "Strike the Shepherd,
> And the sheep will be scattered;
> Then I will turn My hand against the little ones.
> (Zechariah 13:7)

"Yes, I'm the Messiah who was foretold. But I am going to die, and you will stumble." Why did Jesus tell the disciples the good news/bad news? Perhaps because he foreknew their period of doubt and disarray—the bad news. The good news would transcend the bad news. He would see them again after his resurrection.

Our finite minds do not want to listen to the horrific. Perhaps the disciples tuned out the references to death, fearful the last three years would have been for nothing. Jesus knew they would call his words into remembrance, and these times of teaching and the promised Holy Spirit would bring them to victory in their faith. They could believe and trust what Jesus promised would be fulfilled. Their faith would transcend their disbelief.

FOCUS FOR VICTORY

As long as our focus is on the Lord, Faith will come, even if Doubt knocks at our door before Faith tells Doubt to take a hike. Our faith falters when we put our trust in something other than God—such as wealth, power, prestige, or knowledge.

> Cursed is the man who trusts in man
> And makes flesh his strength,
> Whose heart departs from the LORD.
> For he shall be like a shrub in the desert,
> And shall not see when good comes,
> But shall inhabit the parched places in the
> wilderness,
> In a salt land which is not inhabited.
> Blessed is the man who trusts in the LORD,
> And whose hope is the LORD.
> For he shall be like a tree planted by the waters,
> Which spreads out its roots by the river,
> And will not fear when heat comes;
> But its leaf will be green,
> And will not be anxious in the year of drought,
> Nor will cease from yielding fruit.
> (Jeremiah 17:5–8)

For the Christian, faith that transcends is not faith in faith. Rather true faith is a result of changed essence—the essence of Christ through the empowerment of the Holy Spirit.

Now to Him who is able to do exceedingly abundantly above all that we ask or think, according to the power that works in us. (Ephesians 3:20)

JUST A LITTLE FAITH

Faith can still move mountains.

"Just have a little faith." How often have we been challenged with these words? Why is faith so hard to hold unto? Why do we sometimes feel we will never transcend our disbelief?

Now faith is the substance of things hoped for, the evidence of things not seen. (Hebrews 11:1 NJKV)

The heroes of old received what they hoped for because they believed. And because of the certainty of their faith, they ordered their steps according to God's promises and why the mountains moved on their behalf.

Has the church today lost the passion to follow after something promised but not yet seen? Are there no more believers like Elijah, who challenged the prophets of Baal on Mount Carmel? Or are we like the Israelites? Having clearly seen the cloud before us, do we continue to cave at the first sign of trouble? No wonder the world views Christianity as ineffective when those who are called by his name turn tail and run.

If we don't learn to trust God in the morning, how will we trust him in the night?

A LIVING THING

Faith is a living thing. Few believers start out ready to venture across the Red Sea. But God grows our faith through the mundane as well as the miraculous. When difficulty arises, we can either step out on dry land, or we can turn back to Egypt. The choice is ours. But the sooner we claim the faith that transcends, the more ready we become to trust.

Here are a few modern-day faith heroes—stories from author friends who shared their faith experiences for the purposes of this book. While crouched in doubt, their faith eventually transcended disbelief.

By faith, a mother watched her doubtful child release a balloon containing their address into the air. "No one will find this," the child said. The mother encouraged the girl to have a little faith. A few days later the family received a note stating their balloon was found wedged in a fence one hundred miles away. Whenever doubt comes, the mother holds to the memory of the balloon and trusts in the God of the unknown.

By faith, a husband obeyed God's call to start his own business, despite the financial risk, not knowing how he would meet the mortgage payment. God provided, and the couple learned he is the source of their daily bread.

By faith, a friend, who knew nothing about computers, followed God's direction to become a writer. She is amazed at how God has used her words in spite of her limitations.

By faith, one writer enrolled an estranged couple in a retreat and transported them to the event. Because of her faith, a marriage was saved.

By faith, after the deaths of a daughter and a mother within a two-year time span, a woman gave her grief over to God, finding comfort the world could never have provided.

By faith, a wife prayed for her husband's salvation. Through her surgery, God spoke to her husband, drawing him into saving Grace.

By faith, a woman journeyed through the valley of cancer discovering the peace of God that transcends all understanding.

These modern-day faith heroes planted their faith in an unfailing God and the resulting harvest transcended their frail expectations.

> So Jesus said to them, "Because of your unbelief; for assuredly, I say to you, if you have faith as a mustard seed, you will say to this mountain, 'Move from here to

there,' and it will move; and nothing will be impossible for you." (Matthew 17:20)

ELUSIVE FAITH

Even so faith often eludes us.

"Are you up there, God?" That's what my mother used to ask whenever she heard about a child's death or a tragedy claiming multiple lives. She wondered if God was asleep when such things happened. Ultimately, she surrendered to the knowledge of a sovereign God who loves even the sparrow when it falls.

She was not alone in her thoughts. Since time began, those who harbor bitterness toward God perceived they were deserving of only blessings. They argued, "Didn't the Lord say in his word if we obey his commands, our days would be long and prosperous upon the earth?"

My husband's nephew struggled with his wife's terminal illness. She was the glue holding the family together. How could he go on as a single dad with six children, the youngest only seven? He argued with God. "Why my saintly wife?"

On a run, he sensed God's presence as he realized, "How can I accept God's blessings and not the trials?" His journey through this ordeal was a testimony to many of God's grace and strength during hard times. Faith transcended doubt.

A writer friend shared, "After ten years of marriage, we were still an infertile couple. We started the quest to find out why this was happening to us. Then we lost our health insurance, so we couldn't afford to continue with the testing." She states teaching young children in Sunday School was a constant reminder of her infertility, and the thoughts caused her to go into deep depression. One Sunday she came home and cried. Not just a sob but with gut-wrenching pain. "I shouted and kicked and screamed and cried and slammed doors, doubting God even heard one of the thousands of prayers prayed over me down through the years. I doubted all those scriptures about being blessed with children carried any weight. I'd heard them all! And I'd heard the stories of how people miraculously had children after years of trying." She wondered why God singled her out to be barren.

God gave her an answer she did not expect. "I can give you a child right now," he said. "But I will give you hundreds of children for you to influence for my kingdom." God gave her peace and blessings beyond her expectation—his plan far better, though his plan cost her pain. Later, God affirmed this promise when a mother shared the positive influence she gained from my writer friend's story.

What do we do when God doesn't make sense? When he gives a precious gift only to be taken away?

Darlene shares how she too questioned God after her daughter's suicide. He answered her with these statements:

"Be holy because I am holy."

"I am God."

"Because I am God and you are not."

Then the final argument.

"Because I am *your* God."

Therein is the crux of faith. If indeed he is our God, then he is intimately involved in our lives, both its joys and its sorrows. Faith that transcends doesn't need to know the why. Faith that transcends rests simply in the fact God is the great I Am, and the great I Am is our God.

> O LORD, You are my God.
> I will exalt You,
> I will praise Your name,
> For You have done wonderful things;
> Your counsels of old are faithfulness and truth.
> (Isaiah 25:1)

THE UNIQUENESS OF TRANSCENDING FAITH

Victorious faith—faith that transcends—chooses to believe when human reason makes us want to doubt.

Lessons I needed to learn during my cancer journey. I felt weak when I compared myself to so many who'd journeyed this path so victoriously. Could I be brave when I felt so afraid?

One day, while on a comfortable walk with my husband, we stopped at the retention pond near our house and were promptly greeted by happy ducks. I had no bread, but they walked right up to me as if to give me a cheery hello. My husband ran back for duck food and the camera. Two of them were a little hesitant but eagerly gulped down their portions. One little guy, the one who came up to me in the first place, actually ate from my hand. Though they looked alike, each could be identified by the way they expressed themselves in my presence.

"Do you see, Child?" he asked. "If I have created these creatures to be so unique in their personalities, how much more have I fashioned you for my purposes?" As my cancer journey progressed, God continued to pour out his reassurances, helping me to transcend worry.

The symptom of chemo I most feared was the prospect of losing my hair—yes, how vain. I bought a wig in preparation but still feared what was to come. When the first clump fell out, I grabbed my wig and went to the hairdresser. "Shave it off," I said. As I stared at the bald me in the mirror, I laughed until I cried. "Not so bad," I said. A pair of big earrings, and I'm all set."

I knew then, if God could give me a sense of humor over the thing I most dreaded, he'd be with me through the whole process, regardless of the outcome.

Sometimes we feel we have lost faith when we examine our coping against another believer's journey. They seem so much stronger than we are. We ask ourselves if we will ever transcend our fear or be destined to wallow in despair.

There is danger, in comparing our personal situations, whether birth, illness, work, or talents to anyone else. Just as our DNA is specific unto ourselves, so is our faith journey, the one God has specifically designed for each of us.

> But let each one examine his own work, and then he will have rejoicing in himself alone, and not in another. (Galatians 6:4)

I ask the Lord, "Does the fact I struggle to maintain faith mean I am a second-class Christian?"

To measure God's love for us by equal treatment is flawed faith. For if life were fair, we'd all be movie-star beautiful and drive classy sport cars. We seek equality with those who have more, not those who have less. As long as we stay fixated on desiring equal treatment by God, we lose sight of just how much he does love us.

Sometimes I rob myself of true self-evaluation because I'm too busy trying to figure out just where I'm at on the bell curve of spiritual success as compared to those I view spiritually superior. When I look at others' seeming success and blessings, I wonder what God meant when he promised me, "more than I could ever hope or imagine."

In Psalms 73, Asaph states he almost slipped away from God's grace when he compared himself to the prosperous wicked. They seemed to have no earthly struggles and lived like kings. Where were the blessings God promised him? The longer he dwelt on the seeming inequities, his soul hardened, and he describes himself as embittered.

Like Asaph we cry out, "I've done everything you've asked me to do. I'm early to bed and early to rise, but I am far from the promise of being healthy, wealthy, and wise."

Asaph then remembers his relationship with the Lord was far more precious than anything the world had to offer. He remembers the Lord has promised to deal with the wicked in his own time and in his own way. And aren't the wicked as loved by our Father as we are?

As Asaph reasoned the faithfulness of God, he ultimately chose faith and transcended his momentary doubt.

But it is good for me to draw near to God;
I have put my trust in the Lord GOD,
That I may declare all Your works.
(Psalm 73:28)

God's salt transcends when we say, "Today I choose to believe in the midst of doubt and trust him with the rest of my life."

FOR FURTHER STUDY OR GROUP DISCUSSION

1. Read Colossians 3:5.

   So put to death and deprive of power the evil longings of your earthly body [with its sensual, self-centered instincts] immorality, impurity, sinful passion, evil desire, and greed, which is [a kind of] idolatry [because it replaces your devotion to God]. (AMP)

   • How do we deprive sin of its power?

   • How are self-centered instincts such as immorality, impurity, sinful passion, evil desires, and greed a kind of idolatry?

   • By focusing more on the Lord, we rob sin of its power. How can we focus more on the Lord?

2. Read John 4: 46–53.

   So Jesus came again to Cana of Galilee where He had made the water wine. And there was a certain nobleman whose son was sick at Capernaum. When he heard that Jesus had come out of Judea into Galilee, he went to Him and implored Him to come down and heal his son, for he was at the point of death. Then Jesus said to him, "Unless you people see signs and wonders, you will by no means believe." The nobleman said to Him, "Sir, come down before my child dies!" Jesus said to him, "Go your way; your son lives." So the man believed the word that Jesus spoke to him, and he went his way. And as he was now going down, his servants met him and told him, saying, "Your son lives!" Then he inquired of them the hour when he got better. And they said to him, "Yesterday at the seventh hour the fever left him." So the father knew that it was at the same hour in which Jesus said to him, "Your son lives." And he himself believed, and his whole household.

- What had previously happened in Cana?

- Why do you think Jesus responded to the man the way he did?

- The distance from Cana to Capernaum is a little over sixteen miles. For a healthy person, this would be a day's journey by foot, several hours by chariot or donkey. We can only speculate what went through the nobleman's mind as he returned to Capernaum. Perhaps the seeds of doubt had taken root. How did faith transcend doubt?

3. Read Ephesians 1:15–19.

   Therefore I also, after I heard of your faith in the Lord Jesus and your love for all the saints, do not cease to give thanks for you, making mention of you in my prayers: that the God of our Lord Jesus Christ, the Father of glory, may give to you the spirit of wisdom and revelation in the knowledge of Him, the eyes of your understanding being enlightened; that you may know what is the hope of His calling, what are the riches of the glory of His inheritance in the saints, and what is the exceeding greatness of His power toward us who believe, according to the working of His mighty power.

- What does Paul hope the Ephesians will gain from the knowledge of faith in the Lord Jesus?

- Where to wisdom and revelation originate?

- How does this knowledge help the believer transcend difficult circumstances?

4. Read Hebrews 12:1–2.

Therefore we also, since we are surrounded by so great a cloud of witnesses, let us lay aside every weight, and the sin which so easily ensnares us, and let us run with endurance the race that is set before us, looking unto Jesus, the author and finisher of our faith, who for the joy that was set before Him endured the cross, despising the shame, and has sat down at the right hand of the throne of God.

- These verses follow the great list of faith warriors found in Hebrews chapter 11. Jesus is the _____ and _____ of our Faith. In view of this truth, how then should we live our lives?

- How does this knowledge free us to continue in our faith?

5. Read 1 John 5:4.

For whatever is born of God overcomes the world. And this is the victory that has overcome the world— our faith.

- What promise do we find in this verse?

- Have you ever experienced a time when God helped you to overcome or transcend a difficult situation?

6. Read Zechariah 4:6.

So he answered and said to me:
 "This is the word of the LORD to Zerubbabel:
 'Not by might nor by power, but by My Spirit,'
Says the LORD of hosts.

- This chapter describes the futile attempts of the Jews for trying to do things within their own strength. Why do the salt of the Lord keep trying to correct their situations on their own strength?

7. Read Nehemiah 4:1–2.

But it so happened, when Sanballat heard that we were rebuilding the wall, that he was furious and very indignant, and mocked the Jews. And he spoke before his brethren and the army of Samaria, and said, "What are these feeble Jews doing? Will they fortify themselves? Will they offer sacrifices? Will they complete it in a day? Will they revive the stones from the heaps of rubbish—stones that are burned?"

- The Jews were being ridiculed for trying to do the impossible. How does this verse compare with Zechariah 4:6 (previous question). What did happen?

- Are you dealing with a circumstance that seems beyond human ability to resolve? How might these two verses apply to you or to someone you know who is facing a seemingly impossible circumstance?

8. Read Hebrews 10:23.

Let us hold fast the confession of our hope without wavering, for He who promised is faithful.

- The word hope here refers to our Christian hope. What is that hope?

- Who promised this hope?

- How is this deity described?

9. Compare to Romans 5:5.

   Now hope does not disappoint, because the love of God has been poured out in our hearts by the Holy Spirit who was given to us.

   • What hope does the writer of Romans refer to?

   • Why can we rely on this hope?

10. Read Hebrews 10:35–36.

   Therefore do not cast away your confidence, which has great reward. For you have need of endurance, so that after you have done the will of God, you may receive the promise.

   • What confidence is referred to here?

   • From where does this endurance come?

Chapter Eight—Salt Bears Fruit

"We do better by dwelling in the secure place of the Most High than making occasional visits." —Source unknown

Grace is multiplied as we grow in the knowledge of God and Jesus. The better we know God, the more we experience grace and peace.

An animation clip shows a cautious pedestrian waiting at a crossing lane. He pushes the button and waits for the light before crossing. He waits and waits and waits then looks up and down the street several times. Since there's no traffic, he wonders if it is safe to cross. Growing impatient, he steps into the road. Amazingly, the light changes when his foot hits the pavement. At the next stop, the same thing happens, but he tests the pavement a little sooner.

With each intersection, he meets similar success until he skips the rest of the way to his destination. The next day, with no reservations, he steps onto the road, certain the power to change the light was in his feet. He is surprised when he comes head to head with a semi-truck.

This man's dangerous complacency is all too universal. We fall into its pit because we believe the same set of circumstances will bring about the same result. Only when the chair crashes to the floor do we wish we had tested it before sitting down.

THE DANGERS OF COMPLACENCY

Complacency is defined as a feeling of contentment or self-satisfaction, an inability to sense danger. Complacency damages the Christian because our action or inaction is based upon a flawed assumption. Our animated friend was quite content, but his self-confidence led him into a death trap. He put his faith in his own feet rather than in God's power.

God intends for his salt to prosper through the power of the Holy Spirit. Sometimes we fail to grow in our faith, because we become complacent in our walk.

Author Kevin Eikenberry lists five faces of complacency in the corporate world. Perhaps these same truths apply to the Christian experience as well. Scripture may help some with a much needed facelift.

The Champions: Why change the tried and true?

> Pride goes before destruction, And a haughty spirit before a fall. (Proverbs 16:18)

The Resigned: What's the point in striving if the effort won't bring you closer to the goal?

> I press toward the goal for the prize of the upward call of God in Christ Jesus. (Philippians 3:14)

The Comfortable: When life seems good, why change?

> "These things I have spoken to you, that in Me you may have peace. In the world you will have tribulation; but be of good cheer, I have overcome the world." (John 16:33)

The Tired: How can I climb to the heights when I can't even manage the first step?

> We are hard-pressed on every side, yet not crushed; we are perplexed, but not in despair; persecuted, but not forsaken; struck down, but not destroyed. (2 Corinthians 4:8–9)

The Lazy: Why push any harder than what is necessary to get through the day?

> For we are His workmanship, created in Christ Jesus for good works, which God prepared beforehand that we should walk in them. (Ephesians 2:10)

We can avoid complacency by staying close to God. As he breathes in us, we are being continuously changed and readied for eternity. The Israelites had wandered in the desert for forty years. Then God told them to move—to cross the Jordan and claim the promise given decades before. No matter where we are in the sea of complacency, once we set our sights on Jordan, God will pull, push, or prod us out of our complacency toward an ever increasingly vibrant Christian experience.

> The Lord our God spoke to us in Horeb, saying: "You have dwelt long enough at this mountain." (Deuteronomy 1:6)

THE POWER OF THANKFULNESS

One cure for complacency is gratitude. Faith prospers as we grow in appreciation for what God has done for us. And as we acknowledge his grace, we cannot stay in a state of complacency. Gratitude spurs us toward productivity— gratitude energizes.

My kids loved to go to the bank with me because almost every time they were given lollipops. One day the bank gave me two blue lollipops and one red. I had three children to placate. Even if the blue lollipops would have been satisfactory, the fact I had only one red could ignite World War III. Just because there was only one, they all wanted the red. I should have listened to my instincts and left the lollipops at the bank. My children focused on what they could not obtain rather than being grateful for what they could have.

What causes this tendency to focus more on what we don't have than what we do?

Gratitude, according to a branch of science referred to as positive psychology, is an emotion which acknowledges an anticipated or received benefit. Appreciation is experienced if the benefit is perceived as valuable, costly to their benefactor, and given without expectation of return. Thanksgiving is not a feeling of indebtedness. For when one feels obligated, there is a tendency to avoid the giver. True gratitude, however, motivates the recipient to seek out the benefactor and improves the relationship with the giver. According to this school of mental health, a thankful heart is not dependent upon an individual's circumstances. Gratitude transcends negative events within a person's experience and helps us prosper.

If the vinegar of the world sees so much value in maintaining a spirit of being grateful, how much more does God infuse us with a spirit of joy. How much more does our Heavenly Father rejoice in our rejoicing.

Grateful people are happier, less depressed, less stressed, and more satisfied with their lives and social relationships. Gratitude will enhance coping skills when dealing with life transitions or unexpected road bumps. Rather than seek blame, the grateful person focuses on their many blessings.

I ask myself, why does God command believers to acknowledge his goodness? Especially when he doesn't make sense? Why should we offer up thank-you notes in our prayer when we feel God has let us down? How can feeling grateful in the midst of profound doubt help our faith to prosper?

In the days of Moses, God instituted a practice of thank offerings in addition to the sin offerings given by the priests. Why did he do that? God is self-existent, and therefore needs nothing from us.

While God inhabits the praises of his people, perhaps the value of thanksgiving is not for God's benefit but for ours. The New Testament also admonishes the believer to offer thanks to God for our many blessings:

> Therefore by Him let us continually offer the sacrifice of praise to God, that is, the fruit of our lips, giving thanks to His name. (Hebrews 13:15)

Thankfulness keeps the believer centered. Without God's intervention, sin would enslave us. Yet by God's grace, we are free. Because he loved us, he provided a remedy for our sinful natures, the sacrifice of his only son, Jesus Christ:

> For God so loved the world that He gave His only begotten Son, that whoever believes in Him should not perish but have everlasting life. (John 3:16)

The whole gospel summed up in less than twenty-five words.

This is the basis for gratitude. From there, the benefits God gives the believer are endless. Gratitude is the well spring from which our faith grows and prospers.

Gratitude is what gives us the power and confidence to be obedient. Not fear.

Victorious Faith, however, demands gratitude even in those dark holes, those pits where we cannot see him working—those times of hard coping, disappointment, anger, and negativity threatening to rob us of the joy, peace, and love God intends for us.

PROSPERITY OF THE SPIRIT KIND

Gratitude that brings peace and the ability to obey is within the encompassing package of help from the Holy Spirit. This gift is derived not from our own efforts or outward religiosity, rather through faith.

> This only I want to learn from you: Did you receive the Spirit by the works of the law, or by the hearing of faith? (Galatians 3:2)

We still fail to comprehend the depth and width of this faith. These believers' outward behaviors blended in with the rest of the world. I suppose people in Bible times wanted to stay in the good graces of their worldly connections as much as we do today. Paul expressed his sorrow over the believers' resistance to surrender themselves to the filling of the Spirit available to them. Instead, they tried to achieve an outward spirituality through their own efforts. Paul's reminder to be "full of the Spirit" required getting self out of the way in order for the Spirit to do the work. Faith can only prosper as we allow the Spirit to work in us.

We are living carnal, ineffective lives not as the salt God intended, because we do not claim the power of the Holy Spirit—the reason our thankfulness wanes, our obedience fails, and we wallow in complacency.

> For all his days are sorrowful, and his work burdensome; even in the night his heart takes no rest. This also is vanity. (Ecclesiastes 2:23)

The external forces in our lives do not weaken our spiritual walk. Rather, the attitudes we allow to fester within our hearts are the true stealers of God's peace and hampers our spiritual growth. The failure to be thankful, our complacency, is often fostered by emotional baggage put upon us by the world's vinegar.

Hailing from the tundra of the North Country, our years in Florida produced culture shock as I had never experienced before—especially the invasion of fruit flies. I don't know how I've lived so long and not experienced this kind of infestation before our years in Florida. But I had a lot of run-ins with fleas, gnats, shad flies, houseflies, cicadas, roaches, and spiders and determined to tackle this problem. I refused to surrender to a thing so small I could put ten or more on the tip of my little finger. I dug in for battle. I put apple cider vinegar traps around, bought store traps, treated with bleach twice weekly—all the things my research had recommended. Then I went around singing, "Shoo fly, don't bother me."

Two months later, the vermin still thrived.

My anger at these annoying creatures intruded into my everyday life to the point of severe distraction. My self-confidence eroded by an armada of barely visible predators.

While still fuming over the fruit flies, hubs bought me a new computer. Grateful for advanced technology, I struggled with the Thinkpad—over sensitive and not compatible with the way I type. More distraction and self-abasement as I irked my way through multiple deadlines.

That's when the internet went kerflooey.

More distractions, my lack of confidence now fueled by feelings of sheer failure.

Then came multiple health issues, requiring frequent rest breaks, further limiting my ability to meet my tasks.

I argued with God. "I need a little help here. After all, I'm only doing this work for you. How am I ever going to meet the increasing demands on my time and energy?"

When I thought I'd explode from the feelings of helplessness and fear, God pinned me back, as he often does when I think the things I do matter more than whose I am.

He reminded me he's got my back. He knows what things need to be accomplished. And he will be certain those that are truly important get done. Like time with my family and time with my Heavenly Father.

God, in his miraculous timing, brought me to these verses:

Listen to Me, O house of Jacob,
And all the remnant of the house of Israel,
Who have been upheld by Me from birth,
Who have been carried from the womb:
Even to your old age, I am He,
And even to gray hairs I will carry you!
I have made, and I will bear;
Even I will carry, and will deliver you.
(Isaiah 46: 3–4)

Victorious faith—faith that cannot be broken ... faith that thrives and allows us to extend love when doing so seems impossible ... strength in weakness ... confidence in fear ... and joy in adverse situations—victorious faith casts anger to the side and allows us to see as God sees. We are made weak so that he can then make us strong, whether in opposition or circumstances. This is how salt prospers, through the power of the Spirit.

THE SURROUNDING TUMULT

Sometimes we wonder if our faith has root, because our culture seems to be inundated with anti-Christian messages—even to the point of blaming Christians for unrest and division.

In view of seeming increasing attacks, many Christians have succumbed to fear, afraid to speak boldly about their faith. If we surrender to our fear, are we in danger of repeating the very offenses that give credence to these attacks? Some say, "But if we do nothing, we will lose our freedom." But what is the something we must do?

I believe the prophet Habakkuk's words apply today as they did then. He preached before the fall of Judah, in a time of significant moral decadence, perversity, and when war ravaged a nation. He complains to the Lord, questioning his call and purpose. No one listens. Nothing seems to change.

> Why do You show me iniquity,
> And cause me to see trouble?
> For plundering and violence are before me;
> There is strife, and contention arise.
> (Habakkuk 1:3)

"I'm working on it," God says. He reassures Habakkuk God's plan is still the best. Though there will come a time of punishment, Judah will ultimately be restored. Finally, the prophet, though still incredulous as to God's methods, comes to an irrefutable conclusion: even if he is left with nothing:

> Though the fig tree may not blossom,
> Nor fruit be on the vines;
> Though the labor of the olive may fail,
> And the fields yield no food;
> Though the flock may be cut off from the fold,
> And there be no herd in the stalls—
> Yet I will rejoice in the LORD,
> I will joy in the God of my salvation.
> (Habakkuk 3:17–18)

Just as love, goodness, and mercy generate from the Lord, so does peace and spiritual growth. I believe, he stands ready, as he did then, to replace uncertainty with reassurance. He will guide our hearts, our hands, our feet, and our wills toward his perfect peace and help us to thrive.

THE DANGERS OF SPIRITUAL FATIGUE

Sometimes our inability to thrive comes from our exhausted state of being. Just as the world suffers from over productivity, the Christian can become spiritually dry when over extended. We've allowed the world's vinegar—the false sense of perfect productivity—to erode the rest the Spirit provides. We cannot prosper if we are spiritually spent.

Rest can be defined relative to mind, body, and soul: relief from worry; a stopping place; support; tranquility; to be quiet; to rely upon; to belong; to dwell; or to be fixed on something (as in a gaze). Rest is derived from an Old English word used for armor. Wow, what gifts God gives us when we enter into his rest.

Restlessness, on the other hand, means to be in a state of perpetual agitation, an inability to find peace. Restlessness keeps us from feeling God's presence in our lives, from thriving in our relationship with him.

Physiologically, restlessness is often a symptom of sleep deprivation, a relatively new malady in the spectrum of human existence. Before the invention of the light bulb, most humans received a full nine hours of sleep, except for interruptions or stressful events, like a barn burning down. Eventually, things quieted, and one returned to the rhythm of busy days and slumbering nights.

In modern times, millions of Americans suffer from some degree of sleep deprivation. Many Christians blame their exhaustion on being busy for the Lord. God does not want us working *for* him but *with* him—the source of our strength, our durable peace and rest.

For most Americans, sleep deprivation is the direct result of lifestyle choices. Our lust for things to do and things to own fills our activities well into the night. "I'll go to the theater tonight and catch up on my sleep on Saturday," we say. Only Saturday brings its own to-do list, then by Sunday, we either skip church or go with our attitudes wrapped in negative thoughts.

As a medical social worker and family services caseworker, I often encountered patients and clients who suffered significant effects from inadequate rest such as, but not limited to, muscle weakness, pain, hallucinations, dizziness, nausea, tremors, headaches, increased blood pressure, diabetes, fibromyalgia, irritability, memory loss, poor vision, obesity, and symptoms similar to ADHD (attention-deficit hyperactivity disorder) as well as psychosis, stressful relationships, poor performance and, if occurring over a long period of time, premature death.

Why then do we risk our health and pursue things leading to restlessness rather than enjoying the rest we can find in the Lord? Why doesn't rest receive the same significance as food and water? Is our resultant restlessness the reason our spirituality tanks? How can we stay focused on prayer, love others, show compassion, and demonstrate mercy if our brains are flat-lined?

In order for his salt to prosper, God calls us to rest.

"Come to Me, all you who labor and are heavy laden, and I will give you rest. Take My yoke upon you and learn from Me, for I am gentle and lowly in heart, and you will find rest for your souls." (Matthew 11:28–29)

THE DANGERS OF UNRESOLVED CONFLICT

God call us to rest from our bitterness, rage, and judgmental attitudes. We cannot find rest for our souls in the mist of agitation.

In all innocence, John picked the offensive goop off the floor. "Oh, it's a squashed Cheerio," he said. Like a two-by-four from nowhere, the torrent of accusations unleashed. For the next five minutes, his beautiful bride railed about John's insensitivity. She had worked hard all day: cooking and cleaning, running the children here and there, meeting the project deadline at her job. She rails against the first words out of his mouth, perceiving them as condemnation. Hubby bristles at the attack. And so, the stage is set for five hours of ping-ponging blame. And all because of a wayward Cheerio.

Anger, an insidious emotion, can often impede our ability to prosper as God intends for his salt to do. Anger lies buried, simmering and waiting for that explosive trigger to send it spewing unchecked like exploding lava. We read the headlines of unspeakable acts perpetrated as a result of unbridled anger. The escalation of violence in our colleges and schools, restaurants and malls, and our highways and city streets. "Why has the world become so angry?" we ask.

Unrighteous anger leads to distress and stems from many sources. Poverty, injustice, jealousy, and inequality among the most common triggers. But if we go deeper, we see the fuse is not necessarily the external factor but the inward rationale. A sense that hostility toward another is justified because wrong had first been done to us. A false sense we deserve better than we received.

Anger is a common human emotion—one that cannot be denied. Righteous anger does have benefits when channeled productively, perhaps causing changed behavior or a compulsion to right a wrong.

Perhaps the unholy, selfish view associated with anger is the reason Christians deny its existence. I used to think Christians had no business being angry and pushed my rage inward with unhealthy consequences. One day, I realized anger is an attribute of God. And we who are made in God's image are designed with his attributes. The problem is not the emotion, part of the human equation, but our unholy reaction to our anger—the poor choices we make because we're angry.

Just as we physically react to fear, our bodies go through physiological changes when we are angry. The red corpuscles fill up giving us that red glow. Increased adrenaline gives some people superhuman strength. And like fear, continued, unresolved anger is the cause of diseases such as high-blood pressure and gastrointestinal disorders.

Psychologists recommend a process called reframing when we feel ourselves becoming angry. Not to deny the anger but to understand the anger's source and redirect rage toward a positive resolution. If we are angry over a social injustice, psychologists say, we could join a proactive group to affect positive change. If a friend has hurt our feelings, we can let the friend know, affirming how much the friendship is valued. Sequestered resentment is certain to give rise to hostility sooner or later.

If the world can sense the value of finding rest by setting aside our anger and fear, how much more does God want us to resolve our anger and retreat into his rest in order to prosper?

Psychologists also recommend what God has favored from the beginning of time: to forgive. Forgiving lowers blood pressure and eases tension, producing a feeling of good will and relaxation. Anger, like so much negative emotional baggage, keeps us stuck in the mud, unable to prosper in our faith.

Perhaps the best advice in handling anger is from the Great Physician:

> Be angry, and do not sin. Meditate within your heart on your bed, and be still. Selah (Psalm 4:4)

PROSPERITY REQUIRES SURRENDER

Victorious faith requires a surrendering of our wills to God's guidance, especially when life brings vicious winds of change, often beyond our comprehension. If we are unable to trust in God's direction, guidance, and his ability to preserve our purpose, our faith is in danger of withering.

Psalm 1 speaks of two men, two ways, two destinies. One is promised blessings; the other will perish. The righteous man is blessed because he seeks the guidance of the Lord. Not so with the wicked who seek to solve their problems by world standards. God promises the righteous man a life of productivity. He will flourish and yield fruit in season. His faith will endure even in the desert because he is rooted in the Lord. The wicked may appear to prosper for a time but will be blown away by the slightest wind.

During my social work career, I served as the Director of Social Services for an area nursing home. I observed firsthand a dichotomy in the final stages of life. Those who had walked in the counsel of the Lord, or as salt, fared much better against the ravages of old age, even those whose dignities were assaulted by severe dementia. Those who walked in the counsel of the world, living as vinegar, often faced their final days angry, bitter, and alone. Their pursuits were powerless to comfort them in their final days.

Henry's wife was excited when she learned her husband would be joining her in the nursing home. Unable to care for herself following a severe stroke, she entered the nursing home five years earlier. Her needs were greater than her elderly husband could manage, but he visited her faithfully every day.

When Henry realized he could no longer live independently, he agreed to enter the nursing home. Sadly, Henry watched as his life's possessions were sold far below their material worth. He had put his life energy into the accumulation of things. When they were taken from him, he lost the will to live.

The day he arrived, he walked into his room, said nothing, and climbed into bed. He refused to take any kind of nourishment. He died two weeks later cursing the very God who would have been his sustenance if only he would have turned to the Lord for comfort.

Clyde was a man of faith. He had lived in the nursing home ten years before I came to work there. Clyde's humor and zest for living was a refreshing oasis for family members of other residents. Staff often stopped by just to chat. In my first visit with Clyde, he revealed his reason for his joy. "I was a young man when my wife died and left me with seven small children. It was the depression years, and a man wasn't encouraged to be a single father. My family and neighbors tried to tell me to put my children into an orphanage. I just couldn't do it. I'd been a hard-living man until that day. I knelt beside a cow, confessed my sins to the Lord, and asked him to help me be a better man and keep my family together. He answered my prayer. Faith has made all the difference for me."

Two men, two ways, and two destinies.

ADVERSITY: STRENGTH OR DEFEAT?

In the History Channel's mini-series, *The Hatfields and the McCoys*, the end of life is pictured far differently for Randolph McCoy and William Anderson Hatfield. Randolph is portrayed as a devout man who believes in the power of prayer. As violence escalates and spins out of control, Randolph's faith is tested beyond his human endurance, the final blow—the murders of his daughter and son, the senseless beating of his wife, and his home destroyed. These tragedies followed the severed relationship with another daughter and the murders of his three oldest sons. During the attack on his home, he prays for God's intervention. When he views the devastation, he loses his faith. "What kind of God allows this to happen?" he asks. According to legend, Randolph McCoy dies alone in a cabin fire, an alcoholic and embittered man. His faith had been defined by human expectation of deserved preference for a life well lived.

"Devil Anse" Hatfield, or more officially known as William Anderson Hatfield, was a fiercely independent man who lived a hard life. A man who made his own rules in life but a definite leader in his family. Having no faith in the law, he believed, initially, his acts of violence were justified. But others in his family used situations to practice hatred and revenge, going above and beyond the concept of justifiable. Broken from so many losses and tired of bloodshed, "Devil Anse" Hatfield finally seeks God's forgiveness. In the closing scene he is baptized. As he comes up from the water, his hardened face glows with peace.

Why do some believers come through hard times with bolstered faith while others are fatally stung in the swarm of adversity?

There is an innate tendency to believe if we are centered in God's will, if we attend church faithfully, if we read his word, if we practice the tenets of generosity, forgiveness, temperance, and hospitality, then surely the ills of this world will not engulf us. Perhaps that is what Job thought as he made his daily sacrifices for his children, just in case they might have sinned. Yet, Job lost it all, a righteous man who suffered as none has ever known save our Lord. But when the storm clouds settled, Job's relationship with God took on a new depth:

> I have heard of You by the hearing of the ear, But now my eye sees You. (Job 42:5)

Eventually, all Job lost was restored, not from Job's expectation but from God's mercy extended.

We will cease to prosper, if we think we are immune to trials because we are doing his good work. God does not measure his grace to us according to the number of our good deeds, but rather by the degree in which we seek his presence in our lives, regardless of our circumstances.

A friend shared her struggle with discouragement. She wondered why so much adversity blocked her productivity in doing what she believed to be her divine calling. "I no longer wonder if he has called me to write. I know he hasn't. He hasn't called me to do anything in my own strength. He has called me to intimacy with him. Everything else is just the fruit of that relationship ... it is about letting your dreams die and being willing to live out his dreams for you."

She continued, "I can't make God's facts a truth in my life until I believe them. Not just say I believe them, but actually walk in them."

> Indeed we count them blessed who endure. You have heard of the perseverance of Job and seen the end intended by the Lord—that the Lord is very compassionate and merciful. (James 5:11)

PROSPERITY: THE EVIDENCE OF OUR FAITH

God's will for us, his salt, is to bear fruit—to prosper, the evidence of our faith.

> But the fruit of the Spirit is love, joy, peace, longsuffering, kindness, goodness, faithfulness, gentleness, self-control. Against such there is no law. (Galatians 5:22–23)

Although I've read this passage many times, one day God hit me with this truth—fruit is singular. These attributes are bundled as an all-in-one packaged gift endowed by the Holy Spirit. They are promised results when we surrender our hearts to God—the core to our spiritual prosperity. Yet, we try to pick out only the gifts we think we most desire or need, rather than allow the Spirit to work every aspect of God's fruit into our lives.

Though each of us has a different race to run, these qualities are assured for every believer, intended for us to prosper—to bear fruit—for spiritual benefit. God is the perfecter and finisher of each individual believer's race.

> Therefore we also, since we are surrounded by so great a cloud of witnesses, let us lay aside every weight, and the sin which so easily ensnares us, and let us run with endurance the race that is set before us, looking unto Jesus, the author and finisher of our faith, who for the joy that was set before Him endured the cross, despising the shame, and has sat down at the right hand of the throne of God. (Hebrews 12:1–2)

WAX ON, WAX OFF

God fertilizes our souls, not only in times of deep crisis, but through the mundane. In the original movie version of *The Karate Kid*, a teenager and his mother move to California. The boy struggles to fit into his new environment. When a group of karate students bully him, his mother arranges for her son to learn karate from their Japanese landlord, Miyagi.

The lad is eager to learn but becomes confused with Miyagi's methods. He has the teen polish his car. He demonstrates the movement needed to do the best job possible. "Wax on. Wax off," he commands. The boy soon comes to understand, he had learned tremendous skills in performing seemingly senseless tasks; the very skills he would need to defeat his opponents and to prosper.

Likewise, the Lord cultivates the fruit of the spirit within us to defeat the enemy and live victoriously, to prosper.

PROSPERITY IN DETOURS

When I was a child, many times on our trips from Syracuse to visit my grandparents in Northern New York, my father, an avid fisherman, would come upon a dirt road off the main highway. "I think this is a short cut," my father would say as he veered off to explore.

My father's shortcuts often made a trip a few hours longer but always brought excitement to our travels as we traversed through unknown territory never quite certain when or if we'd get to our destination. I always suspected those "shortcuts" were explorations to find new fishing holes.

A wrong turn often is God's intervention. Like my father's hunt for fishing spots, God may have a discovery around the next bend, which we might never have known if it weren't for our lost estate. In this disheartening or adventurous moment, God is shaping us, developing our fruit to prosper us.

On his second missionary journey, Paul attempted to enter Bithynia (Asia) but was thwarted by the Spirit of God (Acts 16:7). Instead, after receiving a vision, he entered into Macedonia, (Europe) preaching in Philippi and establishing an important church there.

While traveling from Northern New York to Florida during the tailwinds of Hurricane Lee, I stayed overnight in southern Pennsylvania. During the night, the entire area was inundated with rain causing wide-spread flooding. I thought for sure, I was trapped when the clerk told me all the roads south were closed. Someone standing nearby mentioned the possibility of one open road. In order to access the highway, I had to backtrack forty miles. I prayed a quick prayer for wisdom, got in my car, and headed toward parts unknown.

In completely unfamiliar territory and with a useless GPS, I forged ahead not really certain where I was or where I might end up when I got to where I didn't know I was going.

When I stopped at a rest area, I met a woman firefighter on her way to New York City to attend the 9/11 memorial events. "It's a trying time," she said, "I hope we make it through. I so need to be there."

"I'll pray for you."

Simple words, but to her, they were laced in gold. She smiled as if a weight had been lifted. Sharing my faith melted those feelings of being lost for I knew my pilot had deterred me for a reason—a chance encounter to let a weary heart know God is able to heal even age-old scars.

Sometimes, he has to make changes in our plans so that he can fit us into his, so he can teach us, mold us, and garden us to prosper, to be the fruit he intends.

> "For My thoughts are not your thoughts, Nor are your ways My ways," says the LORD. (Isaiah 55:8)

FOR FURTHER STUDY OR GROUP DISCUSSION

1. Copy these verses in the space provided. (Use whatever version you choose)

   • Matthew 10:39

   • Matthew 16:25

- Mark 8:35

- Luke 9:24

- Luke 17:33

- John 12:25

- What is the common thread in these verses?

- Why does seeking to serve oneself prevent the believer's prospering in faith?

2. Read Philippians 4.

How do we find peace and rest?
- Rejoice in all _____.
- Know God is _____.
- With _____ and _____ make

your request to God
- Then find Peace that passes

    _____.

- How does the pursuit of peace help the believer to prosper in his faith?

3. Read Hebrews 11:6.

   But without faith it is impossible to please Him, for he who comes to God must believe that He is, and that He is a rewarder of those who diligently seek Him. What components for victorious faith does the author of Hebrews suggest?

   - _____ that He is and is a _____ of those who seek him.

   - Why would it be impossible to please God without faith?

4. Read Isaiah 54:17.

   No weapon formed against you shall prosper,
   And every tongue which rises against you in judgment
   You shall condemn.
   This is the heritage of the servants of the LORD,
   And their righteousness is from Me.
   Says the LORD.

   - What promise does Isaiah give to those who have put their trust in God?

- Why shouldn't we worry about those who might speak ill of us or tell lies about us?

5. Read Joshua 1:5.

No man shall be able to stand before you all the days of your life; as I was with Moses, so I will be with you. I will not leave you nor forsake you.

- What promise can the believer claim?

- Can we claim the promise even when we don't sense God near?

6. Read Psalm 105.

- What are some of the ways God intervened for his people?

- How does this synopsis of Israel's history demonstrate God's desire for his salt to prosper?

- Which verse speaks to you personally?

7. Read 2 Corinthians 11:13–14.

For such are false apostles, deceitful workers, transforming themselves into apostles of Christ. And no wonder! For Satan himself transforms himself into an angel of light.

- How does Satan sometimes disguise himself?

- In what way do false prophets try to drag us back into slavery and prevent God's salt from prospering?

8. Read Psalm 103:10–12.

He has not dealt with us according to our sins,
Nor punished us according to our iniquities.
For as the heavens are high above the earth,
So great is His mercy toward those who fear Him;
As far as the east is from the west,
So far has He removed our transgressions from us.

- How far does God remove our sins?

- Why is this significant?

- If God has removed our sins from our reach to reclaim them, why do we travel back toward them, back to the place where God delivered us?

- How does this prevent us from prospering in our faith?

9. Read Jeremiah 29:11.

For I know the thoughts that I think toward you, says the LORD, thoughts of peace and not of evil, to give you a future and a hope.

- What are the thoughts God thinks toward us? Thoughts of _____ and not of _____.

- What does he want for us? A _____ and a _____.

10. Read Romans 14:8.

If we live, we live for the Lord, and if we die, we die for the Lord. So then, whether we live or die, we are the Lord's. (ESV)

- How does knowing God has control over life or death help us to prosper in our faith?

Chapter Nine—Salt Endures

> For by Him all things were created that are in heaven and that are on earth, visible and invisible, whether thrones or dominions or principalities or powers. All things were created through Him and for Him. (Colossians 1:16)

The long-running reality TV show, *The Amazing Race*, features teams of two who vie to complete a multitude of tasks, detours, and roadblocks around the globe. On each leg, the team who comes in first is not necessarily the strongest or the smartest. Contestants are often waylaid by many unexpected events such as injury, vehicle breakdown, becoming lost, or failure to follow directions. Sometimes tasks take courage—some faint and fail.

In one episode, a team was handicapped by the inability to successfully duplicate an Indian dance routine. Nearly succumbing to the heat and sheer frustration of failure upon failure, the team contemplated giving up. They were so far behind all the other teams they believed themselves to be in last place, and they would face certain elimination. Why go on?

"No. We won't quit," they said. "We came to finish, and that's what we'll do." Depleted of physical strength, the performing member of the team tried the routine one more time and finally succeeded. With heads held high, they crossed the finish line. "I'm not fast," he said, "but I can last."

Unknown to the viewers or the team, the leg was a non-elimination round as long as they completed the tasks. If they'd quit, this certainly would have been the end of the road. By pushing through, they survived to continue the contest several more weeks.

THE BELIEVER'S RACE

As a believer, I am on a different kind of race, as Paul describes our faith journey. He instructs the Christian to run the race with the intent of gaining the prize. For the believer, this is eternal life with Christ. I am reminded of Paul's words at the final days of his ministry, waiting for what he was sure would be execution. Yet, he looked forward to the consummation of his belief.

> I have fought the good fight, I have finished the race, I have kept the faith. (2 Timothy 4:7)

The prize is not for a first-place finish, rather simply finishing the full race. We are not rewarded for our speed but for endurance. The good news is we do not run the race alone. Like the teams in *The Amazing Race*, we have a partner, a wise and competent partner—our captain, the Son of the Almighty God, the Everlasting Father. We can trust his decisions.

He doesn't sit on the sidelines, he runs beside us, picking us up if we fall short. Though we spit and sputter because the race seems too difficult, we can be assured he will carry us to final victory. And when the race is over, he envelops us within his arms. "Well done, good and faithful servant."

> Yet in all these things we are more than conquerors through Him who loved us. (Romans 8:37)

THE OBSTACLE COURSE

Yet, we look to the world's wisdom when faced with obstacles, whether those resulting from poor choices, barriers heaped upon us by other's wrongdoing, or from within, those emotions threatening to bog us down and prevent us from experiencing the victory God intends for his salt.

There is nothing in this temporal world that can separate us from God's saving grace except our own choices. His grace is sufficient to overcome any assault the enemy hurls. He will save us from both our physical and self-destructive stumbling blocks. He will rescue us from all obstacles preventing our closer walk with him—if we ask.

Sometimes we are reluctant to be rescued. We are too tied to the familiar.

Lot was told to flee, but he hesitated. The angels took him by the hand and pulled him out of the city. Even then he argued, wanting to go to another city and a lifestyle he'd favored. Not into the wilderness (Genesis 19).

In order to rescue us, often from our own poor choices, sometimes God gets behind and pushes. Sometimes he pulls us. But he will always be there when we call.

OUR EMOTIONAL OBSTACLES

Sometimes we think we're the only Christians left on earth. Why bother? Who will save us? No one cares. Yet God stands ready to reassure us in the face of our fears.

Elisha's servant was afraid. God opened his eyes so his servant could see the army of God at work (2 Kings 6).

> So he answered, "Do not fear, for those who are with us are more than those who are with them." (2 Kings 6:16)

In a previous chapter, we mentioned how frightened the disciples became when the waves covered the boat. How brave we are in calm waters, and how quickly our confidence wanes when our ship is tossed by the whim of the weather. The world sees the waves and is quick to condemn us for venturing out in the first place.

We often feel tossed about by discouragement, disillusionment, doubt, fear, rejection, and we can only see the vastness of the sea. We feel hopeless. We fear we will be defeated. Satan sends waves intended to make us panic, to forget the God who rescues. Believers have a choice. We can see the waves, or we can see Jesus.

> There is no fear in love; but perfect love casts out fear, because fear involves torment. But he who fears has not been made perfect in love. (1 John 4:18)

We tend to see ourselves as having few resources, failing to realize God has imparted gifts, according to his wisdom, on all his children. How often we second guess God because we feel the task he has given us is unimportant compared to those he has given others. Or perhaps we lack the confidence to pursue the task because we fear God's judgment if we fail. Rather than try, we reject the very gift God has given.

God wants us to complete his plans for us. He has given us his Spirit to endure whatever comes our way, including the unexpected. But not unexpected to the Lord. He knows what lies ahead when we don't.

Perhaps doubt is seeded in our forgetfulness, when we are in the middle between where God brought us from and where he is taking us to. Rarely do segues from one episode of our lives to the next contain beautiful harmonies. Rather, life hits us with discordant perplexes and makes us doubt.

Envy can trigger doubt as well.

One day I golfed at the North Hampton Golf Course near Amelia Island in North Florida. The course links through a posh residential area, the homes upscale and the scenery breathtaking. I was gripped with jealousy, momentary to be sure, but most certainly jealousy. How I'd love to own a home like one of these.

The Spirit pricked my conscience. "I have plans for you," God says. "And I have provided for you. Don't envy these homes, for this is not where I have called you to be. And the place I've brought you to is much better for you."

I realized how shallow envy is, yet how easily envious thoughts can bog us down, eat away at the good life God intends for his salt, and make us doubt God's intentions.

I thought about the children of Israel. We often criticize them for their frequent grumbling and complaining, for their backsliding into idol worship, and most of all for their desire to return to Egypt. We wonder how they could forget they were slaves there. As long as the miracles kept coming, the Israelites praised God. But when faith required patience, choking on the desert dust, thirst and hunger, and facing giants in the Promised Land—they baulked. They envied the very nations God had purposed for them to drive out.

Doubting God's plan for our lives is the soil in which envy takes root. We can only weed envy out by remembering how far God has brought us—believing he will take us the rest of the way to his planned destination.

> Beware, brethren, lest there be in any of you an evil heart of unbelief in departing from the living God. (Hebrews 3:12)

INDESTRUCTIBLE FAITH

Victorious faith transcends envy and doubt because God's mercy endures, his love endures, his faithfulness endures. Because all things begin and end with God, his supremacy makes faith possible.

Faith cannot be broken. We can forget we have this benefit. We can become so fruitless in our circumstances, in torn relationships, in failures, disappointment, doubt, and envy, pulled away by the absurd, we lose sight of our faith. Like a ship adrift whose sailor fails to throw over the anchor. But faith itself cannot be broken. Because faith, like love, endures all things, we can live as pure salt, confident in God's sustaining power.

Linda Wood Rondeau

STRONGER THAN OUR FEAR

Enduring faith is stronger than our fear.

> So Jesus answered and said to them, "Assuredly, I say to you, if you have faith and do not doubt, you will not only do what was done to the fig tree, but also if you say to this mountain, 'Be removed and be cast into the sea,' it will be done." (Matthew 21:21)

I had just settled in to tackle long overdue writing projects when the phone rang. My neighbor had called to give me a heads up.

"Got some bad news to tell you."

I didn't want to hear any bad news, but something told me I needed to. "Go ahead."

"There was another break-in attempt last night."

"On Mother's Day?"

"Oh, yes. About 9:30 in the evening. On the other side of you."

"Alvin and Lordes's house?"

"The rascals cut the wires underneath the meter box, disarming the alarm and power. Then they tried to break-in with a screwdriver. Both Alvin and Lordes were home at the time."

I shivered with the realization. Not only did the attempted robbery happen within a few feet of me, I had been totally unaware what was going on. Blissfully at my computer, I hadn't heard a thing. Not even the police and the power company when they arrived soon after. We laughed over my ostrich lifestyle. My wonderful neighbor said if my house catches on fire, she'll be sure to call me and let me know so I can get out.

I wondered about the brazenness of the potential thieves that night. I realized, because of my inattentive way of life, how vulnerable I am. Fear took root.

When I sat down for my quiet time with the Lord, he had a special comfort for me. I read from Matthew 10:17–31, "Be on your guard against men."

Christ prepared his disciples for ministry. He warned them the road ahead would be full of danger, they would be scorned, arrested, and mistreated. Then he said an amazing thing.

> And do not fear those who kill the body but cannot kill the soul. But rather fear Him who is able to destroy both soul and body in hell. Are not two sparrows sold for a copper coin? And not one of them falls to the ground apart from your Father's will. (Matthew 10:28-39)

He reminded his disciples nothing would befall them without God's watchful eye. Faith endures despite our fears.

After I read this encouragement, confidence dispelled fear.

We have a God who knows our needs, even before we become aware of our dearth or danger. One preacher said, "Perspective liberates us from the urgent." When we realize how precious we are to God, we need not be afraid of whatever man or nature can do to us.

> Do not fear therefore; you are of more value than many sparrows. (Matthew 10:31)

In addition to spiders, I have always had an unnatural fear of bridges.

More than a few years ago, in pre-internet days, when airline tickets were bought from travel agents, I had to pick up our boarding passes in Ottawa, requiring I cross the Ogdensburg-Prescott Bridge. My heart raced before I even got into the car. Remembering perfect love casts out fear, I met the challenge with God's help. I couldn't let my recently widowed mother-in-law spend Christmas alone. With all the determination of a Ruth, I sang "Jesus Savior Pilot Me", took shallow breaths over the water, and shouted a hearty "Hallelujah" when the car rolled past the last span.

Psychologists say fear produces the "fight or flight" autonomic response. Respiration increases causing an auditory gasp. Blood vessels constrict, and we hear our hearts pound. We either engage the obstacle or run from the risk. Staying put only intensifies our physiological reaction.

Franklin D. Roosevelt is credited with saying, "Courage is not the absence of fear." He went on to expound courage is found because something is present that is more important than our fear. Courage, then, is the action we take in spite of being afraid. Courage is when the adrenaline of purpose oils down paralyzing dread and slides us through the ordeal.

The source of fear is often external, forcing us to decide between two undesirable choices. Like the children of Israel, the soldiers advance from the rear while the Red Sea looms ahead. Fear can also be internal, those demons in our past who make our present so terrifying. Sometimes circumstances create a sense of fear because of our poor choices, like the college student who sweats his mid-term because he failed to study.

Sometimes experienced trauma makes us cautious when similar circumstances arise. Caution is not necessarily a negative attribute. As the adage says, "Discretion is the better part of valor." Yellow lights exist for a reason. Gauging the waters temperatures before we take the plunge can prevent hypothermia. But there comes a point when we drown in our caution, too fearful to take that first stroke toward victory.

Sometimes, our fear stems from our feelings of insufficiency. We are mired in our perceived lack. Much like the widow who sought Elisha's help (2 Kings 4). She feared losing her sons to slavery, for her, a fate far worse than starvation. Despite her fear, she opted to trust the man of God and did as he told her and placed her empty vases before her only measure of hope. God multiplied her current resources until the creditors' demands were met, and she lived on what remained.

For the believer, raging streams of fear are eased from the simple reassurance of God's presence. Faith endures despite our fear because God is always with us. He not only stands on our right side, but he is on our left. Like a cloud, he surrounds us, above and below, with his mercy and goodness. He calls us to confidence in his perfect love that casts out fear. Giving us courage to endure.

> Fear not, for I am with you;
> Be not dismayed, for I am your God.
> I will strengthen you,
> Yes, I will help you,
> I will uphold you with My righteous right hand.
> (Isaiah 41:10)

PEACE THAT ENDURES

God provides his salt with enduring faith, resulting in peace stemming from a confidence in our Sovereign God.

> I will lift up my eyes to the hills—
> From whence comes my help?
> My help comes from the LORD,
> Who made heaven and earth.
> (Psalm 121:1–2)

I didn't see them the first few times I walked the corridor. Then a friend who journeyed with me glanced upward. "Oh, look at these tiles!"

We had been visiting a mutual friend hospitalized for cancer treatment. We were worried about her, and our eyes had been cast downward. The strategically placed tiles, painted by children, contained messages of hope, laughter, and occasional scripture reminders. But we couldn't see them without deliberately looking away from our worries. The sight brought us much joy to remember that our dear friend was important to God and tucked inside his palm.

Our perspective improves as we keep our eyes heavenward.

The Psalmist looked toward the hills, the place where sacrifices were made to idols. And he realized he was looking in the wrong direction. So he looked away from the idols to God.

> I sought the LORD, and He heard me,
> And delivered me from all my fears.
> (Psalm 34:4)

The Psalmist was not freed from danger but from anxiety.

OUR PROBLEM FIXER

In a previous chapter, we discussed how God will imbue his salt with wisdom—at the right time and in the right amount (James 1:5), and he dispenses wisdom generously if we ask, "without complaining"

Mental health services are important and help many who suffer from diverse disabilities and clinical illness. God will and does use human resources to meet our needs. We often pray to ask God to lead us to the right physician and to give doctors wisdom in healing our infirmities. For many, however, severe and disabling problems may not be rooted in trauma or mental or physical disability or illness. Sometimes we are emotionally crippled because of selfishness and pride. Sometimes, Christians refuse to get help for fixable situations because they interpret their sadness or symptom to a lack of spirituality.

This truth remains. Whether the solution is found in temporal resources or in supernatural intervention, we can be assured when we seek God's wisdom, he will free us from anxiety and calm the storm. He is the problem fixer. The source of our endurance.

> Now this is the confidence that we have in Him, that
> if we ask anything according to His will, He hears us.
> (1 John 5:14)

Fear, worry, despair, and lingering disappointment are not his will for his salt. The world says, "You should be afraid. You should be angry. You have every right to dwell on this disappointment. They don't deserve your forgiveness. If you forgive them, you are weak."

The Lord's will for the believer, his salt, is to walk in confidence in God's wisdom to face whatever difficulty we confront.

Jesus spent much time with the disciples, teaching them the difference between what the world values and what God wants them to become. Particularly in the Sermon on the Mount (Matthew 5–7), he states, "You have heard it has been said ... but I tell you" (paraphrased).

He showed them the natural world and how God took care of the lilies and the birds. These natural wonders didn't spend time worrying. The God who created them meets their needs.

> So why do you worry about clothing? Consider the lilies of the field, how they grow: they neither toil nor spin; and yet I say to you that even Solomon in all his glory was not arrayed like one of these. Now if God so clothes the grass of the field, which today is, and tomorrow is thrown into the oven, will He not much more clothe you, O you of little faith? (Matthew 6:28–29)

God wants his salt to go to him first. He might point us to simple solutions for our disarray. Yet, he tells us to seek him out, to seek his will and his presence.

CONQUERING DISAPPOINTMENT, DISCOURAGEMENT AND DESPAIR

Psalm 42 describes the cycle of discouragement. If we continue to harbor the anger that accompanies the emotion, we are at risk to experience deep depression. The Psalmist recognized the only hope for his confusion was to call upon the hope that was within him:

Why are you cast down, O my soul?
And why are you disquieted within me?
Hope in God, for I shall yet praise Him
For the help of His countenance.
(Psalm 42:5)

Faith will not be silenced nor squashed into ineffectiveness.

In Psalm 77 Asaph helps us remember the route away from despair.

1. Remember God's greatness as well as his acts of love.
2. Go to God.
3. Remember God's former mercies.
4. Meditate on the positives.
5. Remember God's sovereignty and believe in his love.
6. Trust he will redeem you.

Asaph honestly shares his symptoms. He can't sleep. And he is so down in the dumps he can't even speak. He is exhausted, his thoughts and actions aimless.

Faith that endures will lead us from despair to joy.

We can either focus on the emotion, believe the world's wisdom that it's okay to harbor resentment when the other person is deserving of our ire, or we can focus on God. When we do the latter, we can then apply the gift of joy, peace, and love to propel us into a sense of gratitude and ultimately obedience.

Jacob thought he was marrying Rachel, the woman he loved. He had worked seven long years for his future father-in-law, Laban, a conniver. Yet they seemed like only a few days because he loved Rachel so much. The night of the wedding, Laban makes sure Jacob is drunk so he won't notice the bride he is marrying is actually Leah. By the time Jacob learns of Laban's deceit, there is nothing he can do. Leah is his wife. Duty requires he treat her with the respect a wife deserves.

This is not what he planned.

He still wants Rachel.

Then Laban said Jacob could have Rachel if he worked another seven years. Jacob agreed. Now with the two wives came their servant girls. Thus, Jacob ended up with twelve sons by four women. They became the twelve tribes of Israel. God used Jacob's disappointment to shape the whole history of the Israelite people.

Like Jacob's struggles, the letdown may be an instrument that God will use to forage our futures.

CONQUERING APATHY

Sometimes despair and anger can so erode our purposefulness, we become apathetic.

In the movie *Schindler's List*, Schindler wonders how the prisoner disposing of dead bodies can smile through his tears. "I smile," he says, "because I am grateful, I can still cry."

War and destruction can cause our hearts to stiffen with atrophy. It hurts too much to absorb so much unhappiness, death, and horror around us, the tsunami of humankind's inhumanity. Feelings of helplessness cause us to turn away into a lifestyle of apathy.

Apathy is defined as a state of indifference, an inability to become ruffled or roused to active interest or exertion by pleasure, pain, or passion. Spiritual apathy is a slowing down of vigor and passion for the things of God.

Solomon may be the saddest example of spiritual apathy. While Solomon's early life is filled with remarkable accomplishment, we see the tragic results of apathy in his golden years. His numerous marriages for political gain not only often led to idol worship but also Solomon's active participation. While Solomon never truly stopped believing in God, his passion grew cold. All of Solomon's accomplishments collapsed within a few years of his death.

In a previous chapter, we discussed the dangers of fatigue. Apathy is sometimes caused by physical fatigue. Rest and physical exercise can help invigorate us in those cases.

Sometimes our apathetic state is the result of corporate disinterest. We tend to be like the people with whom we spend the most time. Jamie (not his real name), a young man with high energy, sought the approval of his crowd. While he would prefer to take walks and enjoy nature, his friends wanted to do nothing but sit around, drink, and use drugs. Jamie chose the way of the crowd over his personal preference to appreciate the world God created. He eventually lost interest in taking hikes and wallowed in a non-productive life, losing interest in anything except drinking and drug use.

Most often the root cause of apathy is spiritual dryness, when we've allowed the vinegar of the world to erode our enthusiasm for the things of God. When we fail to stay hydrated, our bodies die. Likewise, if we fail to keep our spiritual beings fed, we will suffer an atrophy of the heart.

In his essay, "Spiritual Apathy: The Forgotten Deadly Sin," Abbot Christopher Jamison says, "We have created a culture of spiritual carelessness that neglects the disciplined life of the soul. This state of mind is often accompanied by statements such as 'I have no time for that sort of thing', where having no time means both not having enough hours in the day and not having the inclination."

Is there hope then? Are we doomed to languish like Solomon? Are we subject to become desensitized, unable to put our anger, despair, fear, disappointments causing our apathy at the foot of the cross?

Faith that endures will eventually bolster, lift us from the pit of "I don't care" to a resurgence of hope.

Some theologians and teachers, like Frederic and Mary Ann Brussat, believe enthusiasm counterbalances apathy and boredom, two common blocks to an engaged spiritual life. Apathy and enthusiasm cannot occupy the same mind.

Perhaps this is why Paul says:

> Rejoice in the Lord always. Again I will say, rejoice!
> (Philippians 4:4)

The word enthusiasm is derived from the roots *en* (meaning within) and *theos* (God). It means having God within or being one with God. People infused with God carry a special kind of energy. They bring warmth and feeling to their relationships and vigor to their activities. If we have lost energy, we can dispel our apathy by surrounding ourselves with people who are energetic. We can throw ourselves into new projects, which will jump start our stalled hearts. Some suggest cranking up the radio and singing our hearts out to the Lord. God won't care if we lack perfect pitch and can only raise a joyful noise.

The cure for apathy is first to recognize we are apathetic. Sometimes we can't taste the vinegar in the salt. We only know the flavor is off. We can only realize our true state as we sit by the waters of God's grace. He will enhance our taste buds to decipher what is off.

> Then I will give them a heart to know Me, that I am the LORD; and they shall be My people, and I will be their God, for they shall return to Me with their whole heart.
> (Jeremiah 24:7)

I am often reminded of the apostle Peter's bad fishing day. I imagine Peter was a fisherman among fishermen noted for his big hauls. Not this day. Not on the shore of Gennesaret. In Luke's account of Peter's call (chapter 5), Jesus saw the two boats. Perhaps Peter's and the Sons of Zebedee's were the only boats on the shore. Perhaps other fishermen made fun of Peter's empty nets.

Then Jesus came, and a large crowd followed him. He asked the fishermen to put the boats out a little from shore where he preached to the throng. When he said what needed to be said, he told them to go to deeper waters and cast their nets. I suppose Peter thought the request absurd.

Perhaps he'd lost heart, become apathetic, saying, "We have toiled all night and caught nothing." (v5).

But because Jesus told him to do this, Peter reluctantly set a course as directed. Imagine his surprise when he caught so many the boat nearly sunk from the weight of the haul (v7). Then Jesus said something even more amazing. "Do not be afraid. From now on you will catch men." (v10) Peter realized his worth to God wasn't dependent upon his success as a fisherman. God had a more important role for Peter. He dropped his nets and followed Jesus, apathy destroyed and hope renewed.

Perhaps, if not for empty nets, Peter would not have known how wonderfully God can fill them.

Paul likewise knew the grace found in weakness.

> And He said to me, "My grace is sufficient for you, for My strength is made perfect in weakness." Therefore most gladly I will rather boast in my infirmities, that the power of Christ may rest upon me. (2 Corinthians 12:9)

ENDURING THROUGH OBEDIENCE AND WORSHIP

In John 14 and 15, Jesus is preparing his disciples for his coming crucifixion and resurrection. He begins the treatise with the famous speech from John 14—don't be troubled. He gives them reasons why they need not let uncertainty rule over them. Later in the chapter, Jesus says:

> But the Helper, the Holy Spirit, whom the Father will send in My name, He will teach you all things, and bring to your remembrance all things that I said to you. Peace I leave with you, My peace I give to you; not as the world gives do I give to you. Let not your heart be troubled, neither let it be afraid. (John 14:26–27)

Jesus tells us these things because he does not want his salt to live in fear, despair, anger, and apathy—emotions that can lead to defeat. He has provided his Spirit, the buoy that keeps us afloat and to experience victorious faith, enduring faith.

Why then do we go around with sad faces and heavy hearts, ready to give up?

Why let sorrow and fear rob us of our intimacy with God?

Faith endures through obedience and worship.

Scripture assures us in heaven we will receive a crown of jewels, and we will be robed in splendor. Sadly, Christians are trying to outshine themselves on earth, more concerned with achievement than relationship. We accumulate instead of forsaking. We cannot worship in spirit and in truth if we are more concerned about the how than the who.

Worship means sacrifice.

The congregation clapped their hands in rhythm to the catchy worship song, "We Bring the Sacrifice of Praise."

I will confess. Sometimes when I prepare to go to church, I feel as though the experience is more an obligation than an inner desire to go to the house of the Lord. Though once I'm there and enter into worship, I'm always glad I made the effort. God never disappoints his children. He is always ready to infuse the heart open to him. This is our victory—our praise.

Sometimes I wonder about the phrase, "sacrifice of praise."

Is praise a sacrifice because it's difficult?

Christians often speak of "praising God," and the Bible commands all living creatures to exalt His name.

> Let everything that has breath praise the LORD.
> Praise the LORD! (Psalm 150:6)

According to various commentaries, there are three different words that are translated "praise" in our English versions. One is *yadah*, meaning "give thanks or confess." A second word is *zamar*, "sing praise." A third word is *halal* (the root of hallelujah), meaning "to praise, honor, or commend." All contain the idea of giving thanks and honor to one who is worthy of praise.

Is praise a sacrifice because it costs us something?

According to some scholars, the terms sacrifice and praise at first might seem to be opposites. We think of sacrifice as offering something at great cost to ourselves. Praise, on the other hand, sounds joyful since the act bubbles from within.

> And now my head shall be lifted up above my enemies all around me; Therefore I will offer sacrifices of joy in His tabernacle; I will sing, yes, I will sing praises to the Lord. (Psalm 27:6)

Perhaps our sacrifice of praise is a response to God who has already initiated our salvation before the foundation of the world. Praise costs us nothing but gratitude.

Is praise a sacrifice because God wants us to be more exuberant?

Does God require us to jump up and down and wave our hands, shout as we might at a sporting event?

In the Old Testament, worshipers came to the temple. And, according to Mosaic Law, made a symbolic act of offering by waving their gifts in front of the altar of God. This was often meat. The offering was released for use of others, often the priests. In so doing, others were blessed by a worshiper's wave offering. (e. g., Exodus 29:24, 26, 27; Leviticus 7:20–34; 8:27; 9:21; 10:14, 15)

Praise that emanates from a joyful heart in turn is used by God to bless others in the corporate worship experience. Joy flowing from the heart can be hand waving or clapping. Often though, the quiet joy we sense can send the Spirit hovering over the congregation. Such is the theme of the chorus, "There's a Sweet, Sweet Spirit in This Place." When we wave our hearts in appreciation of all that God has done, he is pleased. The sacrifice he desires from us is simply being in his presence. When he strengthens us with his Spirit, our faith is restored. Enduring faith transcends whatever baggage preceded our worship. In turn, our praise can minister to others who may need a boost as well.

Is God vain? Does he require our praise for his benefit?

Since God is self-sufficient, he does not require us to feed him. Christians are not meant to form a line of our first fruits and dump our baskets into the mouth of an iron statue. The institution of sacrifice was initiated before the Israelites crossed into Canaan because God knew how fickle their minds were, quickly forgetting the good things God has done, forgetting how many times he delivered them, forgetting that he loved them. Christ's sacrifice and the gift of the Holy Spirit replaces the Old Testament system of sacrifice. But the intent remains the same—so that the worshiper will be reminded of God's love. When we praise the Lord, there is no room for envy, fear, despair, or apathy. God is not arrogant, nor does he need our praise, for all creation sings to him. He commands us to praise, not for his benefit, but for ours so that we may overcome and endure through Faith.

> Therefore by Him let us continually offer the sacrifice of praise to God, that is, the fruit of our lips, giving thanks to His name. (Hebrews 13:15)

FOR FURTHER STUDY OR GROUP DISCUSSION

1. Read Luke 10:38–42.

> Now it happened as they went that He entered a certain village; and a certain woman named Martha welcomed Him into her house. And she had a sister called Mary, who also sat at Jesus' feet and heard His word. But Martha was distracted with much serving, and she approached Him and said, "Lord, do You not care that

my sister has left me to serve alone? Therefore tell her to help me." And Jesus answered and said to her, "Martha, Martha, you are worried and troubled about many things. But one thing is needed, and Mary has chosen that good part, which will not be taken away from her.

- What was Martha concerned about?

- How is this a distraction?

- What was the good part Mary chose?

- How does choosing the good part relate to endurance?

2. Read Judges 6.
   - What question does Gideon ask in verse 13? How does the angel answer him?

   - Gideon looked at his own strength and the strength of his people. The Lord said, "Haven't I sent you?" Why should this be enough?

3. Read 1 Peter 5:6-7.

   Therefore humble yourselves under the mighty hand of God, that He may exalt you in due time, casting all your care upon Him, for He cares for you.

- Whenever we see a *therefore*, the student of scripture should always ask what the word is there for. What does the *therefore* reference in these verses?

- How does casting our cares on him help keep us humble?

- Why should we cast our anxieties on the Lord?

4. Read Psalm 37:1–8.

Do not fret because of evildoers,
Nor be envious of the workers of iniquity.
For they shall soon be cut down like the grass,
And wither as the green herb.
Trust in the LORD, and do good;
Dwell in the land, and feed on His faithfulness.
Delight yourself also in the LORD,
And He shall give you the desires of your heart.
Commit your way to the LORD,
Trust also in Him,
And He shall bring it to pass.
He shall bring forth your righteousness as the light,
And your justice as the noonday.
Rest in the LORD, and wait patiently for Him;
Do not fret because of him who prospers in his way,
Because of the man who brings wicked schemes to pass.
Cease from anger, and forsake wrath;
Do not fret—it only causes harm.

- Peace is part of the fruit bundle given to us by the Holy Spirit. Why should we not worry because some do evil in our sight?

- How does this worry rob us of peace?

- Note that enduring faith allows the believer to transcend worry and overcome troublesome circumstances. Write down the action phrases in this passage, what believers can do through the gift of the Spirit.

- What will the Lord give us in return?

5. Read the following verses and write down God's promise stated in each.

   - Isaiah 40:31

   - Isaiah 41:10

- Isaiah 41:13

- Isaiah 42:16

Read Psalm 4:4.

> Be angry, and do not sin.
> Meditate within your heart on your bed, and be still.
> Selah

- What should we do after we acknowledge our anger?

- How does this wisdom work toward an enduring faith?

6. Read Jude 20–21.

> But you, beloved, building yourselves up on your most holy faith, praying in the Holy Spirit, keep yourselves in the love of God, looking for the mercy of our Lord Jesus Christ unto eternal life.

- Have you ever felt insecure in your own strength but through prayer and reading God's word gained reassurance—your faith strengthened? Write your story.

"Peace is the serenity and confidence that comes from relying on God's word and from looking above circumstances to the One who overrules all circumstances for accomplishment of His own purposes." (a quote from Believer's Commentary)

- Do you agree or disagree? Why or why not?

- How does relying on God's word bring us peace and confidence?

7. Read Ephesians 1:2.

Grace to you and peace from God our Father and the Lord Jesus Christ.

- Where does peace originate?

- The world recommends meditation. How are prayer and meditation different?

8. Read 1 Peter 1:1–2 .

To God's elect, exiles scattered throughout the provinces of Pontus, Galatia, Cappadocia, Asia and Bithynia, who have been chosen according to the foreknowledge of God the Father, through the sanctifying work of the Spirit, to be obedient to Jesus Christ and sprinkled with his blood: Grace and peace be yours in abundance. (NIV)

Benson's Commentary points out Peter is addressing believers dispersed as a result of persecution.

- Do you think they may have experienced fear?

In verse 2 Peter refers to the "elect." These believers are God's salt—those who are called out of the world from a state of ignorance and sin by the word, the Spirit, and God's providence.

- What are the elect called to?

- How are they called?

- What are they given in abundance?

Chapter Ten—Salt Satisfies

"He is the most glorified in us when we are the most satisfied in him."—John Piper

Hunger, as God intended, is beneficial. Hunger is a signal the body needs food. The one who hungers will not rest until the need is met. He who hungers will seek satisfaction before any other human need including sleep and procreation. Hunger propels us into action for we will turn over every stone in our quest for food. If it were not for hunger, we might very well die in our lounge chairs.

SPIRITUAL HUNGER

There is another kind of hunger—a hunger for God. This hunger is as natural as physical hunger. If not for the intervention of the Holy Spirit, the human experience would be in constant search to satisfy a lust for which there is no fulfillment apart from God.

Alienation from God is the consequence of sin. Yet, because we are made in God's image, there is a natural yearning for the Father. Unfortunately, human nature tries to satisfy this natural hungering through pursuits resulting in further alienation—vinegar of the world. Unsatisfied hunger, apart from a relationship with God, may propel us into destructive behaviors, often leading to addiction. Some seek wealth, power, or fame to fill the emptiness. Some ignore the symptoms and pursue a life of apathy. Some seek to assuage a sense of guilt through self-sacrifice. Good deeds fail to dispel the pangs because our motivation is self-centered.

Humanity would be desperate indeed if it were not for God's mercy. Death is deserved, but God's grace is greater than his wrath. He did not leave Adam comfortless and provided a means for reconciliation through the system of sacrifice. At the right time, Jesus became the permanent blood offering for any man, woman, or child who chooses to believe. God welcomes the sinner and says, "I am what you are hungering for. Come to me, and I will satisfy." The believer who hopes in God needs never hunger again, for his supplies are inexhaustible.

Why then do we who are called by his name continue in hunger? What shackles prevent us from being completely satisfied with God's manna? Why do we seek the vinegar the world offers instead of the sweet presence of God?

Five-year-old Bobby broke his fire engine in a fit of rage. Aware he had transgressed, Bobby sought to avoid punishment by hiding his smashed toy in the back of his closet, covering it with his favorite blanket.

Bobby remained downcast the rest of the day. Normally, he would tell his mother about his sadness. She had a way of making things better. What else could he do? Nothing. He stewed in his self-pity. When bedtime came, his mother asked why Bobby looked so sad. Finally, the youngster confessed. Even though he knew there would be a consequence, the strained relationship with his mother was worse than any punishment he could have received. He hungered for a return to his mother's favor. And that hunger determined his actions.

SEPARATED FROM THE SUPPLY

When we falter, we hunger anew for we are now severed from our supplier. Since God cannot commune with the unjustified, the sense of separation is more painful than before we became a believer. God is in the restoration business and stands ready to forgive the penitent. He understands our nature and is ready to renew.

Yet knowing this, many Christians hesitate to return to God in spite of the growing hunger for his presence in our lives. Pride gets in our way. Or perhaps we doubt God's readiness to forgive. We tragically continue in our hunger, settling for Satan's scraps when God has prepared a banquet in our honor.

The Psalmist said:

> As the deer pants for the water brooks, so pants my soul for You, O God. (Psalm 42:1)

The Lord wants us to chase after him in full knowledge he is the source of our spiritual meat, our righteousness.

Have you ever felt hungry, yet stood with the refrigerator door wide open, gazing at the contents, nothing within promising to satisfy? Sometimes we only know we hunger but don't know for what we hunger.

Often our feeling of deprivation is not from a true lack but from what we perceive as lacking. Sometimes, our perceived want is from a misalignment of our spiritual priorities.

HUNGER RESULTING FROM ENVY

Sometimes our perceived hunger is a result of envy. We stand with our assortment of desserts begging God for the same gifts he's given others. We forget he gives to everyone according to his great abundance and his foreknowledge of exactly what we need—at exactly the right time.

We can choose to let our wants trap us in dissatisfaction, or we can turn our wants over to the Great Supplier, who will chisel and shape our desires to align with his will—to make us salt.

HUNGER FROM DISSATISFACTION

Those who hunger will do desperate things until their hunger is satisfied. The prophet Haggai condemned Israel because their hunger was for self which could never be satiated.

> You have sown much, and bring in little;
> You eat, but do not have enough;
> You drink, but you are not filled with drink;
> You clothe yourselves, but no one is warm
> And he who earns wages,Earns wages to put into a
> bag with holes. (Haggai 1:6)

Everyone has experienced a time of intense craving. Like many women, I yearn for chocolate, but the confection only brings a false sense of comfort. Chocolate does not bring me nearer to God, who is the true source of comfort and nourisher of my soul. Not that chocolate in and of itself is sinful—only when I defer to and expect chocolate will comfort me when, in truth, the comfort I need can only be found in the Lord. When I put chocolate ahead of God, I'm choosing vinegar.

When circumstances bring about suffering or pain, sometimes we are driven to religious practices, like chocolate, to provide a form of comfort—wave offerings without the penance and actions that do not satisfy. Without a hunger for God's nearness, instruction, or reassurance, religious practice brings little comfort, a shadow of what God wants to provide to the heart that earnestly seeks him.

During the years following the Exodus, while the Israelites wandered due to their disobedience, they experienced physical hunger. The Lord sent them manna. Each was given all they needed. Manna was an adaptable commodity and could be prepared in a variety of ways, in loaves or cakes or stewed in a pot. Scholars have likened the manna in the desert to bdellium. A thick dark substance resembling chocolate. Bdellium tastes like olive oil and is very fragrant, appealing to the senses.

What God provided was sweet and nutritious and ample. It fell from the sky with the dew without agonizing labor.

The Israelites, however, grew tired of God's provision and began to hunger for their old sustenance, the fruits and meat they had in Egypt. "Wasn't life so much better in Egypt?" they reasoned.

They complained so voraciously, God gave them what they thought they wanted. Quail, day in and day out for a month, until it "came out of their nostrils" (Numbers 11:20). Before long, the manna seemed like a good thing.

The Israelites had been satisfied with the manna until they listened to rabble rousers who spewed discontent, forgetting the steadfastness and faithfulness of God even after their disobedience. The people chose to listen to the rabble, the vinegar, rather than God.

Sometimes, believers succumb to the voice of the Evil One, who will try to convince us we could have so much more if we did not follow God. Satan whispers, "Oh, but you were so much better off before you became a Christian. You were wealthier and didn't have all these rules to follow. You were your own person ..." and the tirade continues until the whisper becomes a roar, and we succumb to the thunder of the Evil One's voice.

THE BLESSINGS OF HUNGER

Jesus reminded his followers how hunger could be a blessing, if we sought the Lord to satisfy that hunger. For if we hunger after God, he has promised to fill us.

> Blessed are those who hunger and thirst for righteousness,
> For they shall be filled. (Matthew 5:6)

Jesus's words are hard to remember when we struggle with disappointment. Instead, we hang up notes of platitudes the world spouts:

- God doesn't close a door, but that he opens a window

- Failure is God's opportunity.
- When man's hope is gone, God's grace is only beginning.

Though I remember all these sayings, I wonder if they aren't just another way we rest on vinegar. When I recall God's many interventions, I am pricked for my lack of memory regarding God's faithfulness.

There is a valley that stretches between God's desires for my life and his fulfillment of promise—in that valley God reveals himself. He stirs my appetite for the good things he has in store.

In Abraham's journey, he kept looking forward to God's promise of a son. Many times, he grew impatient. The longer time passed, the more unlikely or improbable this promise could or would be fulfilled. This delay stretched his faith. At the right time, after decades of pruning, Isaac was born. Yet, Abraham's journey did not end. God still had much more to teach him, as well as Isaac and Jacob and all who followed Father Abraham.

Sometimes our unfulfilled yearnings come from a seeming delay in God's answer to our prayers. Perhaps Abraham's frustration stemmed from only hearing part of God's promise, his sights set on the tangible rather than the intangible elements of God's call, "They will be my people and I will be their God."

Therein is the valley from promise to fulfillment. The wait. In this valley, God teaches us how much he desires to be our God and for us to be his child.

He who overcomes shall inherit all things, and I will be his God and he shall be My son. (Revelation 21:7)

When animals drink, they are vulnerable. Yet their thirst propels them toward the only solution for thirst. We hunger for God because he is the source of all that is worthwhile and nourishing to our souls.

WHO PUT THE VINEGAR IN THE SALT

We all have a longing and desire for something beyond ourselves—the something we lost in Eden. To drink of him means to take him into our life. However, physical thirst is repetitive and can only be satisfied momentarily. Our Savior's living water means we need not thirst again.

This is the call Christ offered to the woman at the well (John 4). The eternal satisfaction for our thirst. The old hymn, "The Crystal Fountain", tells us of this joy, "Where all my soul's deep needs have been supplied."

HUNGER VS WANT

Perhaps we miss this satisfied feeling because we do not recognize the spiritual difference between hunger and want.

Hunger and thirst are driving forces—survival instincts.

Want is a perception of an unmet need. Because we live in the world, we are bombarded with the latest developments and mechanizations of ease. Things the world views as essential. Our want can come from a sense of deprivation as well as the gluttony of overindulgence.

When so many of our friends took cruises, I thought I should have the experience as well. To justify the expense, I booked a cruise to coincide with a writers' conference, bringing along the hubs, of course. God had other plans, perhaps to show me the difference between a want and a need.

Five days before we were to leave for the cruise, I looked at my husband and said, "I can't breathe." An emergency room visit confirmed a diagnosis of severe pulmonary embolism necessitating an ambulance ride to a specialty hospital two hours away.

The boat left without us. Yes, I mourned. The cruise was a loss investment because we did not have trip insurance. When faced with the seriousness of the diagnosis, the cruise faded in importance. My wants and desires changed, and I was grateful the Lord gave us more time together.

Lately, I've noticed a new buzz word on the internet: FOMO

Fear of missing out.

Panic ensues when we feel we might be deprived or miss an opportunity for something good or pleasurable. Our minds tighten, almost like the flight or fight syndrome brought on by a stressful event.

In the movie *Citizen Kane*, the hero is on his deathbed and whispers his last word, "Rosebud." A reporter becomes curious about the last words of a dying tycoon and searches for its meaning. In the end, we learn Rosebud was the name of Kane's sled, the one he had to put aside to earn his way into an apprenticeship—his first step on the road to accumulation of great wealth. The man mourned missing out in the joys of childhood. All his money could not buy back his youth.

We miss out on God's blessing because we fear we might miss out on something else. We hunger for the temporal. We remain hungry because we fail to align our goals with the goals God has for us. To do this, we must be willing to forsake conventional wisdom, the vinegar of the world. Whatever is in the way must go. When Jesus called the fishermen, they immediately dropped their nets and followed him. Though they did not know the future, they were hungry after the things of God. Their perceived worldly need faded in view of the promise of God's fulfillment.

FAILURE TO FULFILL

We mentioned the young ruler in a previous chapter, the one who came to Jesus by night (Luke 18:18–27). Some speculate this man was Barnabas who later became a missionary partner to Paul. This ruler had great wealth and possessions yet felt he lacked something. All his religiosity did not satisfy him. He was righteous, obeying the commandments from the time he was old enough to memorize them. Jesus's remedy seemed impossible to the disheartened man, for he could not see the benefit of the advice. Then Jesus said,

> You still lack one thing. Sell all that you have and distribute to the poor, and you will have treasure in heaven; and come, follow Me. (vs 22–23)

The man went away sorrowful. FOMO made him leave Jesus with his spiritual need still unmet because he had great possessions.

Like the rich young ruler, many of us have impediments keeping us from the satisfaction of a full, rich spiritual walk. Sometimes we don't realize just how hungry we are. We hesitate to free ourselves from the baggage keeping us from knowing what Paul yearned for his fellow believers to experience:

> Oh, the depth of the riches both of the wisdom and knowledge of God! How unsearchable are His judgments and His ways past finding out! (Romans 11:33)

Esau despised his birthright. He was famished. No doubt hunger played at him. Yet satisfying his perceived physical need was more important than his birthright (Genesis 25:29–34). We remain spiritually unfed because we crave the world more than the Lord's benefits, our birthright as God's children.

I got the munchies the other night and opened the refrigerator, poking at leftovers. I started to grab an orange from the bottom shelf, then decided I needed something hot. Soup would be nice. Nope. That would dirty dishes. So I settled for two slices of bread and butter, which failed to satisfy. If I try to substitute something besides what I crave, I end up devouring half the cupboard's contents and still feel wanting.

Hunger generally promotes action. The greater the hunger, the more intense the desire to satiate. But if we are first filled with non-essential nutrients, the brain fails to hear the body's cry for "real" food.

Motivational speaker, Les Brown, states, "Wanting something is not enough. You must hunger for it. Your motivation must be absolutely compelling in order to overcome the obstacles that will invariably come your way." From unlikely beginnings, Brown rose to become a well-known orator. Even as a young child, he saw himself as a motivator. But Brown didn't learn like most children, and the school labeled him as educationally impaired. He states the hunger to be a public speaker burned in him. He refused to give up his dream. Eventually, Brown made a career in broadcasting and is now one of the most highly paid speakers in the nation.

Sometimes we feel dissatisfied because we can't see a larger purpose to our daily routine. We feel we are in a rut, running in unproductive circles, like the proverbial hamster and its wheel.

A Loss of Appetite

Satan will keep us bogged down with the mundane to the point we no longer hunger. Life seems meaningless, so we do not recognize God's greater purpose for our lives.

We fail to act if we sense no hunger.

Perhaps this acceptance of mediocrity, the lack of desire for something better, spills into our spiritual lives as well. We starve spiritually because we don't hunger for the things of God.

Physical starvation occurs when the body experiences a total lack of necessary nutrients. Even the glutton can die of malnutrition, eating much but not what the body needs. If the body does not receive sufficient vitamins and minerals to sustain itself, life ceases. Nutritional deprivation causes fatigue and apathy over time. The starving person becomes disinterested in his surroundings.

Perhaps the same is true of spiritual starvation. Do we stuff ourselves with pleasure and selfish pursuits and leave no room for the meat of God's presence? Have we fooled ourselves into thinking we are satisfied and seek nothing else because we are spiritually malnourished? Have we become content with our discontentment? If we don't feel the pangs, how then will we ever seek the remedy?

Do we sometimes feel empty because we allowed service and works to take the place of our relationship with God? God sought the heart of his people long before he instituted the Mosaic system of sacrifice. He wanted them, not their fruits, vegetables, and animal sacrifices.

> Thus says the LORD of hosts, the God of Israel: "Add your burnt offerings to your sacrifices and eat meat. For I did not speak to your fathers, or command them in the day that I brought them out of the land of Egypt, concerning burnt offerings or sacrifices. But this is what I commanded them, saying, 'Obey My voice, and I will be your God, and you shall be My people. And walk in all the ways that I have commanded you, that it may be well with you.' Yet they did not obey or incline their ear, but followed the counsels and the dictates of their evil hearts, and went backward and not forward." (Jeremiah 7:21–24)

FOR FURTHER STUDY OR GROUP DISCUSSION

1. Look up the following verses. In each, what does God provide in full measure?

   • John 3:16

   • Mark 8:34

- 2 Corinthians 13:4

- Psalm 29:11

- John 10:10

2. Read Mark 8:1–10.

   - What miracle is recorded here?

   - Why didn't Jesus send them away?

   - Compare Jesus's reaction of the hungering crowd to the disciples' doubt?

   - How many loaves to start? How much gathered from leftovers?

Note: Jesus did send them on their way after they were fed. He never leaves his followers unsatisfied.

3. Read 2 Timothy 3:1–7.

   But know this, that in the last days perilous times will come: For men will be lovers of themselves, lovers of money, boasters, proud, blasphemers, disobedient to parents, unthankful, unholy, unloving, unforgiving, slanderers, without self-control, brutal, despisers of good, traitors, headstrong, haughty, lovers of pleasure rather than lovers of God, having a form of godliness but denying its power. And from such people turn away! For of this sort are those who creep into households and make captives of gullible women loaded down with sins, led away by various lusts, always learning and never able to come to the knowledge of the truth.

- Human nature will cause us to only hear what we want to hear. Paul spoke of those who hire and follow leaders who only preach what people want to hear. Is this true today?

- How so?

- How is this spiritually unsatisfying?

4. Read Galatians 5:16–17.

    I say then: Walk in the Spirit, and you shall not fulfill the lust of the flesh. For the flesh lusts against the Spirit, and the Spirit against the flesh; and these are contrary to one another, so that you do not do the things that you wish.

    - How do we control the cravings of the flesh?

    - What does the flesh war against?

    - Why are the flesh and the Spirit "contrary" to one another?

5. Read Psalm 37:1–8.

- What does David warn against?

- Why?

We become envious of others because we hunger over what they have. Sometimes we are envious of evildoers. Not that we want to be evil, but rather we don't feel they deserve the things they have.

- List the actions the Psalmist recommends to align our thoughts and rid ourselves of envy.

6. Read Matthew 8:23–27.

Now when He got into a boat, His disciples followed Him. And suddenly a great tempest arose on the sea, so that the boat was covered with the waves. But He was asleep. Then His disciples came to Him and awoke Him, saying, "Lord, save us! We are perishing! "But He said to them, "Why are you fearful, O you of little faith?" Then He arose and rebuked the winds and the sea, and there was a great calm. So the men marveled, saying, "Who can this be, that even the winds and the sea obey Him?"

Note that the disciples had just recently witnessed a series of divine interventions: the lepers cleansed, the centurion's servant, and Peter's mother-in-law healed along with many other miracles. Yet, the disciples were amazed that Jesus calmed the storm.

- Have you ever witnessed someone else's victory over an illness or trial, yet failed to believe God would do the same for you?

- What causes the believer to be envious of other believers?

7. Read Psalm 128.

- What promise does the Psalmist suggest for those who fear the Lord?

- Is this a guarantee of material gain?

- What is meant by fear of the Lord? How is a fear of the Lord satisfying?

8. Read Psalm 90:13–17.

Return, O LORD!
How long?
And have compassion on Your servants.
Oh, satisfy us early with Your mercy,
That we may rejoice and be glad all our days!
Make us glad according to the days in which You have afflicted us,
The years in which we have seen evil.

Let Your work appear to Your servants,
And Your glory to their children.
And let the beauty of the LORD our God be upon us,
And establish the work of our hands for us;
Yes, establish the work of our hands.

- What does the Psalmist hunger for?

- Why would the Psalmist want to feel glad for the days he was afflicted?

9. Read James 5:7–8.

Therefore be patient, brethren, until the coming of the Lord. See how the farmer waits for the precious fruit of the earth, waiting patiently for it until it receives the early and latter rain. You also be patient. Establish your hearts, for the coming of the Lord is at hand.

- What event is James referring to?

- Do you hunger for the Lord's return?

- What is James instruction for those who are longing for God's appearance?

- Have you ever been so hungry you could not wait for the meal to be prepared?

- How might our impatience for God's coming cause us to stumble?

10. Read Proverbs 1:28–31.

> "Then they will call on me, but I will not answer;
> They will seek me diligently, but they will not find me.
> Because they hated knowledge
> And did not choose the fear of the LORD,
> They would have none of my counsel
> And despised my every rebuke.
> Therefore they shall eat the fruit of their own way."

- What did these people hunger for?

- What is the "fruit of their own way?"

- What is the result for hungering after willful pursuit of our human desires?

- How is feeding the hungry helping the hungry to find the Christ who satisfies?

Chapter Eleven—Salt Overcomes

Get rid of all bitterness, rage and anger, brawling and slander, along with every form of malice. Be kind and compassionate to one another, forgiving each other, just as in Christ God forgave you. (Ephesians 4:31–32 NIV)

Dodging traffic and sniffing dogs, I continued the daily grind going house to house with a grumpy attitude. Hired as a census taker, I trudged through each day unhappier than the day before. Broke, I had taken the job out of desperation. Resentment filled my days as I wallowed in self-pity, bitterness, and anger. I blamed unjust treatment for the dissatisfaction that weighed me down.

What was God doing? Did he require me to leave a good-paying job just so I could shoo away bad-mannered canines? How was I to know God had prepared a blessing in the shadow of shattered dreams? The days had become one woe-is-me-pity-party after another.

The day I met her started out like the preceding ones— void of anything reaffirming. She was a woman about my age. At first glance, I knew something wasn't right. Although cheerful, her words streamed in gibberish phrases. Her handicap forced me to rise above my self-pity and focus on another's need. I thought I was the one reaching out. But her enthusiasm healed me in ways, I could barely comprehend.

She pointed to her head and squeaked out the word, "Stroke." After years working with the elderly, I was familiar with aphasia, the loss of comprehensive speech—sadly a common residual affect following a stroke. Because of this experience, I found ways to communicate with her. Once she understood who I was and why I had knocked on her door, she invited me in. Through stammers, misused words, and speech resembling a toddler's, she explained the huge scar left from the extensive surgery following her stroke.

She smiled and said, "I not to live!" Then she showed me how well she could walk. She rejoiced in the gains she had made from an injury that should have taken her life. Amazed, I wondered how she maintained such cheerfulness given the disabilities she now faced. With a smile that would light up Chicago, she said, "God—good! Better me than dead!"

What wisdom—exactly what I needed to hear that day.

FAITH REMAINS WHEN ALL ELSE IS GONE

No matter what tragedy comes our way, we can still be grateful we are alive. To be human is to have trouble. And those troubles may throw us into turmoil. But as long as the believer has breath, God is greater than the burdens we carry.

Faith is more precious than gold. Though durable, gold is not indestructible. But faith remains when all else is gone. Faith not only endures—faith overcomes.

His divine power has given us everything we need to live a Godly life.

> Blessed be the God and Father of our Lord Jesus Christ, who according to His abundant mercy has begotten us again to a living hope through the resurrection of Jesus Christ from the dead, to an inheritance incorruptible and undefiled and that does not fade away, reserved in heaven for you, who are kept by the power of God through faith for salvation ready to be revealed in the last time. In this you greatly rejoice, though now for a little while, if need be, you have been grieved by various trials, that the genuineness of your faith, being

much more precious than gold that perishes, though it is tested by fire, may be found to praise, honor, and glory at the revelation of Jesus Christ, whom having not seen you love. Though now you do not see Him, yet believing, you rejoice with joy inexpressible and full of glory, receiving the end of your faith—the salvation of your souls. (1 Peter 1:3–9)

God is not merely in the business of preservation—he intends for his salt to thrive. In order to thrive, he has provided the sustenance we need. Not just to endure but to overcome the emotional and physical obstacles to an abundant life.

> The thief does not come except to steal, and to kill, and to destroy. I have come that they may have life, and that they may have it more abundantly. (John 10:10)

THE VALLEY OF LONELINESS

God intends for our paths to be filled with his goodness. To this end, he has promised to level the rough ways, to help us overcome the trials, tests, and human frailties the world might use to sweep in and crumble our paved roads into stony trails.

> Every valley shall be filled
> And every mountain and hill brought low;
> The crooked places shall be made straight
> And the rough ways smooth. (Luke 3:5)

Rugged ways can suddenly appear as a result of our bad choices or from other people's insensitivity and ill-will. Often, our steps can become unsure through life's experiences and how we choose to cope.

Sometimes the Lord allows us to experience places of desolation. We all feel lonely at some point in our lives. God created us to be social beings, and we need human contact beyond ourselves. One of the most frequent complaints of being widowed or divorced is the absence of a loved one's touch.

All of us are vulnerable, from the youngest to the oldest, from the richest to the poorest, from the most privileged to the most destitute. Loneliness knows no social classification. Even Christ, the Prince of Heaven, felt the pang of loneliness on the cross when he cried, "My God, my God. Why have you forsaken me?" (Matthew 27:46).

Loneliness is more than the feeling of wanting company. Indeed, many report feeling lonely in the middle of a crowd. Alarmingly, loneliness is one of the key challenges facing college students. Loneliness is a feeling of being cut off, disconnected, and alienated from other people.

Recent studies have classified loneliness as the cause of many illnesses, certainly an enhancer of heart disease, including high blood pressure. Weight gain, sleeplessness, and premature aging are only some of the resulting physical impacts of prolonged loneliness. People who are lonely are also vulnerable to depression with accompanying feelings of uselessness and hopelessness.

Feelings of loneliness can result from the dread of being alone. Some people cannot cope with themselves as their only company. Perhaps the reason some need to have the television, radio, or other musical device blaring at top volume during those times they are by themselves.

Even the most devout believers experience feelings of isolation. Troubles found in the hailstorms of life can obliterate our usual bridges. We find ourselves in an emotional, physical, social, and sometimes spiritual wasteland.

Prolonged loneliness can lead to despair.

Psychologists offer some worthwhile, although world-wisdom, tips to help cope with feelings of loneliness including professional counseling, medications, or structuring lonely days by taking a class or pursuing a hobby. Psychologists also point out being alone doesn't necessarily equate to being lonely.

Scientists may have discovered a genetic fingerprint that partly explains why persistent loneliness is unhealthy. Researchers aren't saying genes doom some people to loneliness and others for rich relationships. Rather the loneliness-gene research suggests certain genes may be more or less active in lonely people, thus compromising the lonely person's health.

Some psychologists have suggested the importance pets may have for chronically lonely people. Research indicates pets reduce factors such as high blood pressure and triglycerides. Surprisingly, even robotic dogs bring benefit to the lonely and isolated.

THE UNSEEN BENEFITS OF LONELINESS

Sometimes loneliness can be beneficial. The distaste for being alone may propel us to seek out something new or different, to explore paths we never thought possible or even desirable.

> "Pray that your loneliness may spur you into finding something to live for, great enough to die for." (Dag Hammarskjold, Swedish Statesman and United Nations official, 1905–1951)

Loneliness, like many of life's discomforting experiences, can provide opportunity.

Anna, widowed after only seven years of marriage, found herself cut off from the life she expected. During her long widowhood, she never left the temple, but found purpose in prayer. And because of this passion in her life, at the age of 84, she was present when Simeon officiated over Christ's circumcision. Anna, in her loneliness, drew closer to God. In turn, generations have been blessed by her story. And she, along with Simeon, prophesied to "all who looked forward to the redemption of Jerusalem" (Luke 2:38).

Loneliness is sometimes viewed as a barrier to success or fulfillment. But with God's enlightenment, that wall falls and becomes a bridge to untold blessings.

> I have set the LORD always before me; Because He is at my right hand I shall not be moved. (Psalm 16:8)

THE VALLEY OF DISAPPOINTMENT

As with loneliness, victorious faith provides the means to overcome disappointment.

A little girl approached author Carol Howell (Senior Life Journeys) during a recent talk. "Remember, Mrs. Howell," the sweet innocent said, "God won't put any more on you than you can handle."

"Oh, Kayla," Carol said. "That's really not a biblical concept. God will definitely put more on us than we can handle. He does so in order to make us turn to him. What comforts me, is the knowledge God will not put more on us than he can handle."

Kayla, like many believers, had the misconception if we are true believers, God will not allow anything to happen beyond our ability to cope. Disappointment tests our faith, and we ask, "Where were you God? Why did you let this happen?"

Disappointment is part of the human condition as much as loneliness, anger, grief, and a myriad of debilitating emotional reactions to life's circumstances. Who among us has not felt disappointment to some degree? Even Jesus experienced the pain of rejection by those he loved.

Many cases of disappointment are caused by what psychologist call cognitive dissonance. This occurs when expectation is incongruent with reality. When our desire or object of pursuit exceeds the bounds of reality, defeat is likely and can lead to disappointment.

Ultimately disappointment is not what truly matters but how we process these times.

Great writers and thinkers have a lot to say about this concept:

> If we will be quiet and ready enough, we shall find compensation in every disappointment. —Henry David Thoreau

> Disappointment to a noble soul is what cold water is to burning metal; it strengthens, tempers, intensifies, but never destroys it.—Eliza Tabor

Disappointment cripples the soul when we believe we are deserving of a particular outcome. When life does not curve the way we want or if we don't receive what we feel we deserve, we give up and become enslaved in disappointment's domino effect: I expect what I think I deserve, I don't get it, I feel disappointment. As a result, I feel less capable or confident or strong and then I feel discouraged or even depressed. This cycle has no good outcome and can lead to severe mental or physical health issues such as chronic depression or high blood pressure.

Does this mean we shouldn't try?

No. That's sour grapes.

Like Aesop's fox who couldn't reach the grapes, we leave the situation feeling defeated. We rationalize the perceived failure with the thought, "Wasn't meant to be." Or we go look for that proverbial window when the door closes. We think our problem-solving approach is at fault. We fail to recognize perhaps the fallout is God ordained. Or if not God caused, certainly something God can use in our spiritual discipline.

BEAUTY IN UNREACHABLE GRAPES

God has created us as unique individuals with different characteristics. We often make the mistake of expecting the same outcome as someone else who may have traveled a similar path, and we fail to take into account our different makeups, our peculiar God-made construction.

We become frustrated when our visions and reality seem unable to mesh.

I enjoy watching the Olympics, though I'm not a sport enthusiast. These dedicated athletes work their whole lives in hopes of achieving the gold, feeling as though the silver or bronze is not enough. During one swimming event, I watched a one-time champion turn sorrowful eyes toward his teammate who prevailed. The gold had been but a breath away. But like that instant between sleep and wakefulness, someone snatched victory from his grasp. Someone else reaped the glory while he would forever remain someone who also swam.

Like a raised scar, a scathing loss never leaves us. And the pain is real. Often times, though, the sting of disappointment is eased through God's redirection in our lives.

We waited anxiously for word on our loan request. The home seemed perfect. We were fast outgrowing our tiny trailer, and we desperately wanted a yard where the children could play. When the bank turned down our request for a seemingly stupid technicality, we were devastated. Two weeks later, my husband changed jobs requiring a move to a different city. The house would have been a stumbling block to the move. God sometimes disrupts our plans because he has other plans, better plans than we could have ever thought possible.

In a popular Christian song, "Day Star Shine Down on Me", the songwriter asks God to make him a reflection of God's light. In the chorus, the songster remarks how God can make the wrong thing right. Redirection from disappointment brings blessings otherwise never to be experienced.

When disappointment comes, we do a have choice. We can wallow in despair. Cry, "Foul! Unfair!" We can vent our anger and seek revenge upon the one who wronged us. When we fail to meet our own expectations, we can flail ourselves with emotional insults. Or we can seek God's council in the face of disappointment. We can trust his redirection.

The Valley of Adversity

Like loneliness and disappointment, Satan will use adversity to attempt to erode our faith.

Conflict. Conflict. Conflict. That's the mantra of the fiction writer. Take your characters, make them uncomfortable, and turn up the heat. Like an overtaxed character, we wonder why life must be so complicated. Can't we just finish out our days on a warm sunlit beach, stretched in our lawn chairs? No job hassles, no family issues, no teenagers to worry about.

Good Opposition

As much as our human nature detests the uncomfortable, opposition can be a good thing. Adversity heightens our awareness and drives us from our complacency. God allows complications in our lives, not to relish in our discomfort like the tortured character of a thriller, but to help us grow and seek God's intervention. For when we look back, we can say as the prophet Zechariah:

> "Not by might nor by power, but by My Spirit," Says the LORD of hosts. (Zechariah 4:6b)

Such was the case with Nehemiah, an Israelite prophet during the period of the Babylonian captivity. Nehemiah was the king's cupbearer. Definitely overqualified for his position, Nehemiah was educated and sensitive. He might have better served the king as a scholar or advisor. Instead of grieving his underappreciated status, he served the king faithfully and won his favor. When Nehemiah became burdened for the condition of his homeland, his countenance changed.

The king noticed, even though Nehemiah said nothing, and permitted his return to Jerusalem, equipping him for the task of rebuilding the wall.

Yet, Nehemiah's challenges had only begun. There were those who viewed a renewed Jerusalem as a threat to acquired power. They orchestrated a four-pronged attack against Nehemiah's vision: physical, mental, social, and spiritual, even before the first brick was laid.

"Give up, Nehemiah," some said. "God has forgotten you" "God has changed his mind" "You've bitten off a whole lot more than you can chew."

Nehemiah held fast to what he believed to be God's will for his people. Instead of taking adversity to heart, Nehemiah prayed. As he prayed, his confidence increased (Nehemiah 4:6). In spite of false flattery, duplicity, and personal attack, he overcame the impossible in a phenomenal fifty-two days (Nehemiah 6:15). Even if using today's technology, the feat was beyond human endeavor. Nehemiah did not put his trust in men but in God.

When faced with a God-given, seemingly insurmountable task, the world would not condemn us for abandoning our goal when attacked from all sides. Satan's taunts purposefully make us feel overwhelmed or incompetent. As Nehemiah learned, we can be confident when facing adversity. God has already paved the way for success. Otherwise, why would Satan torment us?

> Blessed is the man who endures temptation; for when he has been approved, he will receive the crown of life which the Lord has promised to those who love Him. (James 1:12)

THE VALLEY OF BITTERNESS

Bitterness will erode the believer's spiritual vitality. Bitterness is often the result of unresolved disappointment and adversity. Our human nature will, of course, be vulnerable to bitterness when external forces thwart our desires.

WHO PUT THE VINEGAR IN THE SALT

Like the fabled fox mentioned earlier, we sit in full view of what might have been. We determine what we wanted probably wasn't any good. If only the fox had given the Maker a chance. Maybe God would have sent a mouse to add those few extra inches, and they could have shared a feast.

Sometimes we become bitter because of betrayal, multiple losses, or spiritual letdown. We think God has left us, or we fear he doesn't care about our problem.

Diane (not her real name) thought she had a wonderful marriage. Then she learned her husband had a platonic affair. The other woman began stalking her husband, arguing with him, and haunting their lives. The husband became frightened and in a moment of weakness, murdered her, believing this was the only way to protect his family from her insanity—a real life *Fatal Attraction*.

Diane's husband admitted his guilt and was sentenced to life in prison.

Devasted, angry, and bitter, Diane filed for divorce.

Then faith took hold, and she began visiting her husband. She forgave him, and they remarried. While they hoped for parole, Diane found a purpose in this tragedy and was able to minister to women in like circumstances. Soon she began appearing on talk shows and started writing about her experiences. Her testimony of how God helped her triumph over bitterness has touched thousands of hearts.

We allow the trap of bitterness to overtake us because we think our issues and tears are too trivial. Yet when one of our children run to us for comfort from a tiny scratch, we are pleased to wrap them in blankets of our great love. How much more love God has for us.

We become bitter because we doubt or do not accept God's waiting arms.

THE VALLEY OF COMPLACENCY

Just like disappointment leads to bitterness, our spiritual walk can become stalled because of complacency. Where apathy stems from a sense of uselessness, complacency lulls us into a sense of false security. We are content. Why wish for more?

This lukewarm approach to our spirituality is what Jesus condemns in the Church of Laodicea.

> I know your works, that you are neither cold nor hot. I could wish you were cold or hot. So then, because you are lukewarm, and neither cold nor hot, I will vomit you out of My mouth. Because you say, 'I am rich, have become wealthy, and have need of nothing'—and do not know that you are wretched, miserable, poor, blind, and naked. (Revelation 3:15–17)

Complacency robs us of the ability to recognize our need. We continue believing everything is hunky dory. We have no need to read the Bible because we believe we have no problems. We don't pray because we believe there is no need to pray. The result is a distancing from God's spirit. We are falling headlong into a pit and don't even know we are falling.

THE VALLEY OF UNRESOLVED GUILT

Victorious faith—faith that overcomes—will move us from guilt to the knowledge of God's complete forgiveness.

Two men were on trial for armed robbery. As the eyewitness took the stand, the prosecutor moved about the courtroom.

"So you say you were at the scene when the robbery took place," asked the prosecutor.

"Yes," said the eyewitness.

"And you saw a vehicle leave?"

"Yes."

"Did you see the occupants?"

"Yes. Two men."

"And are they in the courtroom now?"

Just then, the two men raised their hands, ending all doubt as to their guilt.

The world detests the word guilt. In our feel-good society, we strive to ignore or redefine guilt, that uncomfortable feeling we have done something wrong. We choose to blame others or use the excuse our poor behavior was a compulsion, something over which we had no control. We dislike guilt because guilt incriminates. Like the famous Edgar Allan Poe story, our own beating heart condemns us.

Guilt is a basic human experience but runs the gamut as to how people cope with the emotion. According to some psychologists, the expression of guilt will vary from person to person. In some cases, guilt will lead to improved behavior. While in others, guilt eats away at their soul, and the smitten can find no peace.

Sometimes we own guilt we do not deserve. Like Robert Barone in the television series, *Everybody Loves Raymond*, we walk into a room armed with a predisposition we will garner disapproval.

GOOD GUILT?

Similar to fear and anger, guilt can be a useful emotion when tempered by a right relationship with God. For guilt that comes from conviction, a loving slap to our souls sent by the Holy Spirit, is the means by which God woos us. Without a realization of our need, we would not seek forgiveness. With forgiveness comes release.

For those who believe, there is a remedy for guilt. For once we have acknowledged our sinful state, God has promised forgiveness. God does not leave us to wallow in our failures, real or imagined.

> For all have sinned and fall short of the glory of God, being justified freely by His grace through the redemption that is in Christ Jesus.(Romans 3:23–24)

Why then, do we insist on carrying our guilt like bricks around our necks? Too often, Christians fail to claim the forgiveness God offers. By ignoring his provision, our continued guilt keeps us hostage, making us spiritually ineffective.

God's forgiveness is complete and eternal:

> There is therefore now no condemnation to those who are in Christ Jesus, who do not walk according to the flesh, but according to the Spirit. (Romans 8:1)

TWO KINDS OF GUILT

There are two kinds of guilt that impede our ability to overcome. There is perceived guilt—guilt we own but don't deserve. Every time it rains, I know I caused the downpour. The kind of guilt that makes you check your speedometer whenever a police officer whizzes by—you are sure he is after you. There is an old adage that says: "If the shoe fits, wear it. If it doesn't, throw it out." We need to examine the source of our guilt feelings. We need to learn to forgive ourselves when we fall short—when we have to throw out the cake because we forgot the baking powder. These are merely mistakes.

Then there is guilt from sin. That guilt feeling is the pulling of the Holy Spirit convicting us of our sin and lingers until we come to the throne of Grace and seek forgiveness. The good news is we are justified freely by his grace through the redemption available through Christ Jesus, who has paid the price for our sin—for all time.

God's forgiveness is complete and eternal.

> For Christ also suffered once for sins, the just for the unjust, that He might bring us to God, being put to death in the flesh but made alive by the Spirit. (1 Peter 3:18)

Christians have difficulty understanding the completeness of Christ's forgiveness for the past, present, and future. We agonize over our spiritual failing instead of asking for forgiveness so we can learn and move forward. Satan wants us to perceive ourselves as miserable failures in our Christian walk. He wants us to wallow in our guilt rather than throw ourselves upon God's mercy—mercy the Lord has promised to extend to us.

GOD'S MASTER PLAN FOR ALL OUR VALLEYS

Before the world was made God knew Satan would fall and man would follow him in sin. And he had already prepared a master plan. This plan has been worked out in the incarnation, death, resurrection, ascension, and glorification of Christ.

In the Old Testament, the priest could only enter into the Holy of Holies at designated times of the year and only through a ritual of approach. Because of Christ's work, we have the privilege of entering God's presence 24/7. Yet we persist to live as unforgiven, downtrodden, discouraged, beaten, angry, and feeling hopeless—unable to approach God.

God wants to forgive us our failings, restore us to fellowship once again, and help us overcome the obstacles keeping us from being the salt he desires for us to be.

FOR FURTHER STUDY OR GROUP DISCUSSION

1. Look up the following definitions and write them in the space provided.
   - Complacency

   - Apathy

- Cynicism

- How are these attitudes similar?

- How are they different?

- Is it harmful to expect the worst of others?

- Are believers vulnerable to the above attitudes?

Now look up the definition of the following words and write them in the space provided.

- Endurance

- Prosperity

- Overcoming

- How are these elements of victorious faith similar?

- How are these elements different?

2. Read Romans 15:4–5.

    For whatever things were written before were written for our learning, that we through the patience and comfort of the Scriptures might have hope. Now may the God of patience and comfort grant you to be like-minded toward one another, according to Christ Jesus,

    - Where is hope found?

    - Who gives us the power to overcome?

    - How are hope and overcoming found?

    - Some translations use endurance rather than patience. How are these concepts similar?

3. Read James 5:11 in several translations.
    - What word is used in place of endurance?

    - How is steadfastness similar to endurance and overcoming?

4. Read Colossians 1:10–12.

So as to walk in a manner worthy of the Lord, fully pleasing to him: bearing fruit in every good work and increasing in the knowledge of God; being strengthened with all power, according to his glorious might, for all endurance and patience with joy; giving thanks to the Father, who has qualified you to share in the inheritance of the saints in light. (ESV)

Compare with other versions.

- What other words are used similar to overcoming?

- How does overcoming bring about patience?

- How does overcoming bring about joy?

5. Read Proverbs 24:10.

    If you faint in the day of adversity,
    Your strength is small.

    - What application do you see to the believer's journey of faith?

6. Read Psalm 119:169–175.

    Let my cry come before You, O LORD;
    Give me understanding according to Your word.
    Let my supplication come before You;
    Deliver me according to Your word.
    My lips shall utter praise,

For You teach me Your statutes.
My tongue shall speak of Your word,
For all Your commandments are righteousness.
Let Your hand become my help,
For I have chosen Your precepts.
I long for Your salvation, O LORD,
And Your law is my delight.
Let my soul live, and it shall praise You;
And let Your judgments help me.

- Where does the Psalmist find understanding?

- How do Scripture reading, prayer, and praise promote a faith that overcomes?

7. Read 1 Thessalonians 4:7–8.

For God did not call us to uncleanness, but in holiness. Therefore he who rejects this does not reject man, but God, who has also given us His Holy Spirit.

- How is living a holy life possible?

Human degradation is the result of a mind distanced from God's purpose for creation.

- Do you agree or disagree? Why or why not?

- How does knowing God's purpose for his salt help our faith to overcome?

8. Read Psalm 46:1–3.

> God is our refuge and strength,
> A very present help in trouble.
> Therefore we will not fear,
> Even though the earth be removed,
> And though the mountains be carried into the
> midst of the sea;
> Though its waters roar and be troubled,
> Though the mountains shake with its swelling.

Benson Commentary: God is our strength to bear us up under our burdens, and to fit us for all our services and sufferings ... the Hebrew word ... *gnezra nimtza meod* ...or a help found exceedingly or accommodated to every case and exigence whatever.

Barnes Commentary: The word rendered "present"— נמצא *nimetsa*—means rather, "is found," or "has been found;" that is, he has "proved" himself to be a help in trouble ... rather, that "he has been found" to be such, or that he has always "proved" himself to be such a help, and that, therefore, we may now confide in him.

- What is the difference between self-confidence and confidence in the Lord?

- According to the Psalmist, why should we not fear these calamities?

9. Read Hebrews 3:14.

For we have become partakers of Christ if we hold the beginning of our confidence steadfast to the end ...

- How is confidence essential to faith that overcomes?

- Where is our confidence found?

10. Read Hebrews 4:16.

Therefore let us [with privilege] approach the throne of grace [that is, the throne of God's gracious favor] with confidence and without fear, so that we may receive mercy [for our failures] and find [His amazing] grace to help in time of need [an appropriate blessing, coming just at the right moment]. (AMP)

- What is the relationship between prayer and confidence?

- Why should we not be afraid to approach God?

- How does remembering our position as salt work toward faith that overcomes?

Chapter Twelve—Salt Rejoices

Rejoice always, pray without ceasing, in everything
give thanks; for this is the will of God in Christ Jesus
for you.(1 Thessalonians 5:16–18)

The story is told about a man who fell into a hole. Three
men came by. The first man was a teacher and scolded the
man for his lack of knowledge. He should have seen the
hole and not fallen into it. The second man was a preacher.
He told the man he'd come to this predicament as a result of
his sin. The third man, a traveler like himself, jumped into
the hole. "Why did you do that," said the one who'd fallen.

The traveler looked at the man with great compassion.
"Because I've been in this hole before, and I know the way out."

The man rejoiced for he was finally free from captivity.

For the Christian, the traveler is the Lord. In a previous
chapter we referenced the fruit of the Spirit (love, joy, peace,
longsuffering, kindness, goodness, faithfulness, gentleness,
self-control), and this gift was shown to us through Christ's
example.

> For to this you were called, because Christ also
> suffered for us, leaving us an example, that you
> should follow His steps:
>> "Who committed no sin,
>> Nor was deceit found in His mouth";
> who, when He was reviled, did not revile in
> return; when He suffered, He did not threaten,
> but committed Himself to Him who judges
> righteously; who Himself bore our sins in His
> own body on the tree, that we, having died
> to sins, might live for righteousness—by

whose stripes you were healed. For you were
like sheep going astray, but have now returned
to the Shepherd and Overseer of your souls.
(1 Peter 2:21–25)

THE VINEGAR IN OUR JOY

God desires his salt to know complete joy in our relationship with him, as Christ found joy in his relationship with the Father. Scripture gives us three commands to assure our hearts will not atrophy, to continue in joy as we grow in the Lord. Rejoice—pray—and give thanks.

If we are filled with the Spirit, there is no room for things or attitudes that can rob us of the joy God has in store for us. A Spirit-filled life is a fountain bubbling over with joy. As the old Sunday School song goes, "I've got the joy, joy, joy, joy, down in my heart."

The devil seeks to erode this joy through our insecurities, anger, and anxiety.

Previously, we discussed how the Lord provides for us to be overcomers, to prosper, and endure to the end. Through all this, God sustains our joy.

Sometimes our joy is eroded because we hug to a wounded spirit. Our anger, bitterness, disappointment, and despair may be evidenced by conversation riddled with negativity or judgmentalism. We might even shudder when an idea or an individual's name is expressed. We want justice rather than restoration.

These feelings are common to all humankind. Especially when our sense of fairness is challenged. In and of ourselves, we cannot feel joy when so much of the world is besieged by evil: wars, starvation, child suffering, human trafficking, lewdness, and a world seemingly run amok.

Yet, the command is clear:

Enter into His gates with thanksgiving,
And into His courts with praise.

Be thankful to Him, and bless His name.
(Psalm 100:4)

We can still know his joy though surrounded with adversity, sin, and seemingly incongruous circumstances because Christ is the source and subject of joy, Christ is in control of our circumstances, and he lives within us.

While disillusionment can erode our joy, sometimes we allow self-hatred to pierce our hearts. Some have perverted John 12:25—

> He who loves his life will lose it, and he who hates his life in this world will keep it for eternal life.

—to mean we should abase ourselves to find favor with God.

This thought has permeated the history of religious practice. The flagellants beat themselves to the point of scaring to show their utter contempt for their flesh. People would fast for long periods of time or practiced self-deprivation to the point of near death, not out of love to God but because of pure hatred for themselves. Some feel they cannot approach God, believing all flesh is evil.

Some have perverted the command to love others as themselves to mean we should despise ourselves. If this is true, how then can we relate in love to others? Satan would have us hate ourselves to drag us into despondency and steal our joy.

> For all the law is fulfilled in one word, even in this: "You shall love your neighbor as yourself." (Galatians 5:14)

To hate one's life means to love Christ more than one loves his own interests—to replace the love of the temporal with the yearning for God's infilling. The world teaches we should look to our own interests first. We ask ourselves what will paying close attention to the things of God cost me?

For the believer, to hate one's life does not mean to adopt a sense of worthlessness. We are Christ's possession, salt, bought with a price—his dear treasure. To hate one's life means to embrace Christ first—to place him in the center of our decisions before our physical comfort or convenience—to find satisfaction, our joy, in him through the power of faith.

WHERE JOY IS FOUND

Our joy is found in this truth:

> Stand fast therefore in the liberty by which Christ has made us free, and do not be entangled again with a yoke of bondage. (Galatians 5:1)

Christ has set us free from self to find joy in the pursuit of serving others.

> For you, brethren, have been called to liberty; only do not use liberty as an opportunity for the flesh, but through love serve one another. (Galatians 5:13)

Therein is our joy. We cannot wallow in self-pity when we think of others' needs before ourselves.

JOY IN THE MIDST OF GRIEF

Satan wants to rob us of joy by focusing on self. He will intensify our sadness especially our grief. He will prolong our sense of deprivation and use whatever tricks he can to prevent us from knowing God's peace and joy in the midst of our loss.

Joy does not necessarily mean clapping our hands, jumping up and down in excitement. Sometimes joy is simply the confidence that God is active in and through this difficulty. Allowing him to guard our hearts against the risks of prolonged sorrow.

> Be anxious for nothing, but in everything by prayer and supplication, with thanksgiving, let your requests be made known to God; and the peace of God, which surpasses all understanding, will guard your hearts and minds through Christ Jesus. (Philippians 4:6–7)

"I don't understand," I told my friend. "When Dad passed away, I mourned but not for a long time. Why is it so hard to get over my mother's death?"

Like many people, I thought grief could be measured like days, weeks, and months. I wanted to take a pill and get over the uncomfortable feelings. In reality, grief is not something we get over. Loss is permanent. But we can get through the pain of change and emerge stronger through faith. Our joy can be renewed. Once I stopped trying to "get over" my sorrow on my own strength and gave my grief to the Lord, my heart began to mend.

Any loss can cause grief, including loss of a personal relationship, loss of physical health, loss of income, loss of financial security, or the loss of freedom. Seemingly less significant issues may cause us to mourn such as: moving away from home, changing jobs, selling the family home, or retirement.

Grief hurts. The body may go through a host of physical reactions such as fatigue, nausea, lowered immunity, weight loss or weight gain, aches and pains, and insomnia. Initially, one may feel shock or disbelief, then profound sadness. Some experience intense guilt over words said or not said, actions taken or not taken, and feelings felt or not felt. Significant loss may trigger intense fear. Some are angry and direct their anger toward God. One mourner confessed, "I shook a fist at God for five years."

Psychology experts suggest many ways to cope with grief—chiefly: laughter, rest, relaxation, counseling, and acknowledgment of the hurt we feel. There are grief support groups available in most communities. Hospice also offers bereavement services. While these resources are helpful, the believer has the additional, more powerful, help from God, our comfort and healer. He has promised to restore our joy. The pain we feel is not evidence of a lack of faith unless we allow the pain to keep us from the One who has the answers.

Linda Wood Rondeau

COMFORT FOR GOD'S SALT

Jesus understands our loss, because he himself experienced loss. Though divine, he became flesh and willingly surrendered to indignities of the flesh. His obedience led to his death on the cross. (Philippians 2:6)

Isaiah 53 shows us how the Messiah would die to alleviate our grief. Other scriptures tell us that Christ binds up our wounds. The Hebrew words translated as "bind up" means to "wrap around." Christ wraps his Grace around us like a blanket of love.

Though we may never know the why, we know the Who.

> For we do not have a High Priest who cannot sympathize with our weaknesses, but was in all points tempted as we are, yet without sin. (Hebrews 4:15)

The church sign says, "Smile, God loves you." An overused phrase, perhaps, but I wonder if as believers we forget this basic truth. Why have we let the mundane and the dreary rob us of our joy? Why do we forget that we are the Beloved's and the Beloved is ours?

I must confess, there are days when choosing joy is difficult—much easier to wallow in my self-made bog of defeatist attitudes. Then the Lord reminds me of a lesson he taught me years ago:

I had just put the misappropriated toy gun back on the shelf and scolded my son. "No, ask first." At three years old, he should know better than to put things into the cart without my permission. I continued my grocery shopping trying to forget, at least for the moment, that I was destitute.

An unemployed, single mother of three, I believed, until that morning, I had already sunk to the bottom. Now I was faced with possible eviction, not from my wrongdoing, but because my landlord wanted to use my apartment for someone else. I had nowhere else to go and envisioned myself among the homeless. Would I lose my children if I had no roof over my head? Self-pity filled me. Trenched in a sour mood, doubt became my war buddy. I felt justified in my feelings of defeat.

After putting the baby in one cart, I lifted the other two children into another and choo-chooed my way through the supermarket, a maternal steam engine with a trailing caboose. I unglued my eyes from my grocery list just in time to witness my son dump a handful of candy bars into the cart. My howls echoed through the store like canyon winds. "What are you doing? Don't even think you're getting candy!"

Feeling like Snow White's evil stepmother, I heaved the treats back on the shelf. Wet trickles slid down my cheeks as my child's little face turned from rosy innocence to gray fright, his wails even louder than my reprimands. Like an out-of-body experience, I saw myself in frozen ugliness, and I wondered if this was what a nervous breakdown looked like.

Staccato-like bursts of joy pierced my nightmare. I reeled to find their source. No one around except a near hysterical, rotund man, a department store Santa type even sporting a long white beard and black boots but sans the red suit. What nerve to find pleasure in my pain! But as I passed from participant to observer, I realized how absurd I must appear. Soon, my own giggles sprayed the atmosphere like a happy geyser.

I don't know how, but somehow time stood still for the Santa look-alike and me. But when the bustling resumed, despair was replaced by a cotton-cloud of peace. I remembered God's promise that he would never leave me forsaken. Despair gave way to hope and hope to joy. Within a few days, I did procure another place to live—not without a few mountains being moved in order to obtain the housing.

God sometimes sends his angels at times when we least expect. Was the odd, obese man on the supermarket bench, one of these times? Had I been so graced? I won't know this side of heaven for sure. But when sorrow crowds my day, I'm reminded of that fat elf, and I am filled with joy unspeakable.

> Sing praise to the LORD, you saints of His,
> And give thanks at the remembrance of His holy
> name.
> For His anger is but for a moment,
> His favor is for life;
> Weeping may endure for a night,
> But joy comes in the morning. (Psalm 30:4–5)

Job grieved like no one else in the Bible. He lost everything but his life. In the end after all the world's wisdom, the vinegar of philosophies, arguments, condemnations, and questions, Job simply says:

> "I know that You can do everything,
> And that no purpose of Yours can be withheld from
> You.
> You asked, 'Who is this who hides counsel without
> knowledge?'
> Therefore I have uttered what I did not understand,
> Things too wonderful for me, which I did not know.
> Listen, please, and let me speak;
> You said, 'I will question you, and you shall answer
> Me.'
> "I have heard of You by the hearing of the ear,
> But now my eye sees You.
> Therefore I abhor myself,
> And repent in dust and ashes." (Job 42:2–6)

Through his grief, Job saw God's majesty and power. This is the source of joy—a Sovereign God loves us so intimately.

FOR FURTHER STUDY OR GROUP DISCUSSION

1. Read Matthew 15:28.

   Then Jesus answered her, "Woman, your faith [your personal trust and confidence in My power] is great;

it will be done for you as you wish." And her daughter
was healed from that moment. (AMP)

Here Jesus heals the woman's daughter. We know
sometimes, even though our faith is great, the prayer for
earthy healing doesn't always happen.

- How does knowing God's sovereignty help the
  believer in coping with profound loss?

2. Read Matthew 11:29.

   "Take My yoke upon you and learn from Me, for I am
   gentle and lowly in heart, and you will find rest for
   your souls."

   - Rest is essential to heal from any injury—physical,
     mental, or spiritual. How does learning from
     Jesus help us to rest?

   - Have you ever experienced a time when God
     called you to rest?

   - What did you learn from the respite?

3. Read 2 Corinthians 1:6.

   Now if we are afflicted, it is for your consolation
   and salvation, which is effective for enduring the
   same sufferings which we also suffer. Or if we are
   comforted, it is for your consolation and salvation.

- That God allows suffering is hard for believers to understand. How can we rejoice when in adverse circumstances?

- Have you ever been comforted by someone who endured a similar affliction?

- How does knowing we are not alone in our suffering help us to rejoice?

4. Read Psalm 42:5.

   Why are you cast down, O my soul?
   And why are you disquieted within me?
   Hope in God, for I shall yet praise Him
   For the help of His countenance.

Look up: Psalm 42:11, Psalm 43:5, Psalm 71:14, Psalm 84:4.

- How does remembering the Lord's goodness bring us from mourning to rejoicing?

The Psalmist struggled with times of deep distress. Life was filled with many struggles. The promise of God's presence raised his spirits and gave him hope.

- How is it possible to rejoice in the midst of great sorrow?

5. Read Revelation 22:4.

> They shall see His face, and His name shall be on their foreheads.

This verse, of course, speaks of our future hope to see Christ face to face. Many verses point to the knowledge of our future hope as a basis to rejoice.

- Why is this? How does this knowledge ease current pain?

- What are ways God "shows his countenance" to us here on Earth? (Review the verses from Psalms in number 4.)

6. Read Psalm 103:12.

> As far as the east is from the west,
> So far has He removed our transgressions from us.

Read this verse from the hymn, "It Is Well with My Soul."

> My sin—oh, the bliss of this glorious thought—
> My sin—not in part but the whole,
> Is nailed to the cross, and I bear it no more,
> Praise the Lord, praise the Lord, O my soul!

Tradition says Horatio Spafford was inspired to write the song after his daughters died in a shipwreck. When heard by a man who suffered great financial loss in the panic of 1899, he exclaimed, "If Spafford could write such a beautiful resignation hymn I will never complain again." The hymn has inspired many over the years.

- Why do you think inspiration is found in the above words?

- How does this verse compare with Psalm 103:12?

7. Read 1 Peter 1: 3.

Blessed be the God and Father of our Lord Jesus Christ, who according to His abundant mercy has begotten us again to a living hope through the resurrection of Jesus Christ from the dead …

- What does "living hope" mean? How does Christ's resurrection give us this living hope?

8. Read Ephesians 1.

God is our Father. This implies intimacy. God is also high and above human comprehension. Our spiritual blessings are a result of our union with God through Christ. We receive this favor as a believer in his son, Jesus Christ.

- Why is this something to "get all excited" about?

In verse 4, we are told God desires believers to know they are a chosen people, a royal priesthood, a holy nation.

- Why is this something to "get all excited" about?

9. Read Ephesians 1:2.

Grace to you and peace from God our Father and the Lord Jesus Christ.

- Look up the meaning of rejoice and write it in the space provided.

- How are peace and rejoiceful similar?

- What is the origin of peace and rejoicing?

10. Read 1 John 4:4.

   You are of God, little children, and have overcome them, because He who is in you is greater than he who is in the world.

   - What do you do to show your pleasure when the team you are routing for is victorious?

   - Why should we rejoice when facing struggles not of our own making?

Chapter Thirteen—Victorious Faith Loves

By this we know love, because He laid down His life
for us. And we also ought to lay down our lives for
the brethren. (1 John 3:16)

We'll never have perfect knowledge this side of Heaven,
but we can have perfect love. Love is the greatest gift and
the practice of love will keep us from misuse of knowledge
or skewered interpretations. Love begins with God and is
given to his children, his precious salt.

God calls his salt to abundant living—to transcend the
bog of the world's vinegar. Faith begins with acceptance
of the vast, imponderable, and complete love the Father
bestows. We cannot truly love others, until we allow God's
love to fill us.

GOD LOVES YOU

Because we abide in Christ, God's love resides in us, a
power we often fail to tap. We, being of the earth, cannot
fathom how a Holy God can live within our crumbling flesh.
Yet he does.

As we measure our days, I hope we will do so by the
measure of God's grace that he freely gives to us each
morning. We do not honor God's love when we dwell on
our failures, especially after we've confessed them.

Yesterday's failures are yesterday's failures.

If God has forgotten them in the sea of his forgetfulness,
then why do we remind him? God wants us to claim his love

and start each day fresh with him. Why is this truth so hard to believe? Why do we hesitate to hold his outstretched hand?

> My flesh and my heart fail;
> But God is the strength of my heart and my portion forever. (Psalm 73:26)

Love Abides in the Midst of Crisis

Why do we doubt God's love in the midst of crisis?

Susan's soldier husband has been slain in active duty. John has been fired after twenty-three years of faithful service. Miranda's only child took a job in faraway Singapore. Ernie entered a nursing home when his daughter could no longer care for him. These people have experienced life-changing events and are in crisis.

Even good changes, such as a new job, college, or a family addition, will cause panic and stress. How do we cope when night and day are indistinguishable and acids slosh in the stomach?

The Genesis Prescription for Stress Management

Genesis proves God is able and desirous to move us from chaos to order, to bring us through any crisis in our lives—big or small in our own eyes—and to remembrance of God's love.

"In the beginning, God ..."

All things begin and end with God the Father. No more theory, no more argument. Simply that God is, God does, and we are his.

He will order our days.

People in crisis often report an inability to sleep. Exhaustion leads to deteriorating health. The first step to recovery is to separate our mornings and evenings according to their functions. Morning is for awakening, the time when the light brings the world into focus. Light reveals our imperfections as well as our strengths. Darkness quiets—a time to forget and a time to dream.

In his wisdom, love, and caring, God will move us forward.

As we move forward, the cloud of our crisis event begins to take form.

When God divided the land and sea, he gave earth definition. A dear friend recovering from cancer told me she coped by making sure she had a reason to get up each morning. Even simple goals such as watering plants can shake the dust from our feet and give us purpose, a reason to praise. From praise, we gain strength.

By ordering the celestial bodies, God created the seasons. Likewise, in his great love, he has planned the seasons of life for the believer, his salt. Each season seems to blend into another. Yet, each distinguishes our activities accordingly. God brings order from our chaos, laying seeds and then bringing these to bloom on his timetable.

Creation was both progressive and preordered. God has been at work in our crisis, even though we may not have recognized his presence. He is preparing us for the day when he says, "Go, now. And inhabit what I have made for you." He has brought us from confusion to dreams, from visions to productivity, from labor to purposefulness, and from fruit to habitation—all that is needed to bring us alive in him.

God rested because he had finished his work. He calls us to rest from our burdens. We have crossed the threshold of crisis. Our transition is complete and through his love we find peace.

THE POWER TO LOVE

Oh, how Jesus prayed for us to understand this all-surpassing love.

> And I have declared to them Your name, and will declare it, that the love with which You loved Me may be in them, and I in them. (John 17:26)

This power, given to us through the Holy Spirit, enables us to understand God's love and to truly love others, to transcend our crisis, to use our growth through the crisis to minister to others.

Love transcends inconvenience. The Spirit at work within us enables us to provide an emotional hug even at our most importune times.

Because I had been inconvenienced, God provided an opportunity to share a blessing, one I'd have missed if I had remained focused on the difficulty the situation created for me. After already deplaning once due to mechanical issues and waiting on the runway another hour, we were asked to deplane again. By this time, I'd missed my connecting flight, and the staff worked feverishly to make other arrangements. I was given one of two last available seats at the rear. My seatmate also had been inconvenienced getting the last available seat next to me. As we talked, I learned she was on her way to see her father who was dying. I was able to pray with her, and she moved from visible anxiety to peace.

All one has to do is turn on the television, go to a social media website, or pick up a newspaper, online or in print, to see the evidence of humankind's inhumanity toward one another. Shootings, rages, crimes, and assaults seem epidemic. Yet within these events, God has sent his heroes. I wonder if these heroes were placed in hard circumstances to illuminate the power of God's love.

I think of the young man who publicly expressed his forgiveness toward the confused police officer who shot his brother. At the moment of the officer's sentencing, this young man demonstrated a love only possible through God's power within him. His tearful, "I forgive you," touched a nation.

LOVE IS SACRIFICE

When we realize how much we have been forgiven, is there any wonder God commands us to love as he has loved us?

> A new commandment I give to you, that you love one
> another; as I have loved you, that you also love one

another. By this all will know that you are My disciples, if you have love for one another. (John 13:34–35)

In the children's classic story, "The Velveteen Rabbit," a stuffed toy wants to be real. At first, he sits on the shelf with the other toys. When the boy becomes ill, the rabbit is given to him for companionship. In the course of time, the rabbit shows the impact of wear and tear. His beautiful fur is torn and matted. When the boy's health improves, the rabbit is tossed aside and forgotten. The rabbit only becomes real through sacrifice.

Unconditional love, the love Christ extends to us, the love he wants his salt to extend to others, may sometimes hurt, is sometimes unappreciated, and often quickly forgotten. Yet love, Christ-like love, undefiled and pure, dusts the world with flavor, the kind people everywhere hunger for.

Christ-like love is more than a handshake on Sunday morning. More than a dutiful card shower to a sick friend. Christ love is tested, endures, and is witnessed through a myriad of thankless thoughtfulness.

LOVE CONQUERS ALL

Even the world realizes hatred is a damaging emotion. Crimes committed in the name of hate and senseless animosity toward a class or race of people, bear a worse penalty than perhaps what might be dubbed a general crime of passion, a rash act perpetrated against someone in the heat of the moment prompted by intense emotion such as jealousy.

Hate, the antithesis of love, is not an emotion we are born with. Hate is often learned or the result of trauma. Hate is birthed from anger or a strong dislike of someone or a group of people. Unresolved, these feelings can intensify, becoming wrath. While some would say anger and wrath are synonymous, wrath denotes a fiercer emotion or anger on steroids. A definition of wrath is: "Strong, stern, or fierce anger; deeply resentful; indignation or ire; vengeance or punishment as the consequence of anger."

Left unchecked, as the above definition implies, wrath can lead to violent outbursts or purposeful malice toward a person or group, symptomatic by blasphemy or strong intemperate language and bitterness that saturates one's thoughts.

In the package of the fruit of the Holy Spirit, love includes the power to overcome hate and is the greatest of all the Spirit's benefits:

> And now abide faith, hope, love, these three; but the greatest of these is love. (1 Corinthians 13:13)

John also stresses the importance of love, especially among believers. Love is the undeserved embrace of God for his dear people—a super affection. God desires his salt to show this God-love to others.

The world toots a horn and says, "More love." But this kind of love is man-generated, rarely lasts, and is artificial. We try to generate this love by thinking good thoughts of others or doing good deeds for the less fortunate. This is not the kind of love John instructs believers to demonstrate. Believers are God's arms and feet in a broken world. The kind of God-love believers should demonstrate is God-endowed through the work of the Holy Spirit. Salt, like the Velveteen Rabbit, is willing to love sacrificially.

Only through grace can the believer move from anger to love.

The world justifies anger against injustice or social indifference to suffering. And the Lord hates evil. But as a Holy God, his wrath is righteous. Human wrath is often dangerous, even though we feel our reactions are justified.

Most often, anger is fueled by personal assault or betrayal. While the world will say we have a right to be angry, the Apostle Paul advises:

> Be angry, and do not sin: do not let the sun go down
> on your wrath. (Ephesians 4:26).

Anger is a human emotion and can propel us toward change when tempered by love.

Humans fail to comprehend God is sovereign over injustice. Many are trapped in doubt at this seemingly inconsistency and ask, "How can a Holy God allow atrocity?"

When Jesus was arrested in the olive garden, one of the disciples drew a sword and cut off a soldier's ear. Christ had just prayed, asking God to preserve his disciples through the horror of the next few hours and beyond, knowing persecution and unjust treatment would be part of the Christian experience. Paraphrased, Jesus rebukes the disciple, "Don't you think I could call out and 10,000 angels would come to my rescue? They who live by the sword shall die by the sword." (Matthew 26: 47–55)

The crowd that had so recently waved palm branches and hailed him as a king would soon cry out for him to be crucified. Knowing the rejection ahead, Christ still journeyed to the cross. This was his sacrificial love. The Christ-like love the Spirit imparts to his salt.

The Spirit works to imbue the believer with holy attributes. We are being made in God's image, and we are sometimes incensed at injustice. Rightly so. However, God is still sovereign and owns the right to equate justice in and through his terms.

> Beloved, do not avenge yourselves, but rather give place
> to wrath; for it is written, "Vengeance is Mine, I will repay,"
> says the Lord. (Romans 12:19).

His methodology of dealing with inequities is incongruous with the world's wisdom regarding anger. Human anger is defined as a very powerful emotion stemming from feelings of frustration, hurt, annoyance, or disappointment—a normal response ranging from slight irritation to strong rage.

God desires his salt to submit aroused anger to his sovereignty, not to ignore our very human side of indignation. Suppressed anger is destructive, often the basis of anxiety and depression. Anger inappropriately expressed or ignored can destroy relationships, affect thinking and behavior patterns, and create a variety of physical problems. Chronic (long-term) anger has been linked to health issues such as high blood pressure, heart disease, skin eruptions, and digestive disorders. In addition, anger is often the root to felonious crimes and domestic violence.

Even the world recognizes the harmful effects of anger if not correctly managed. Conventional psychology suggests many methods of dealing with anger such as deep breathing, positive self-talk, or channeling angry thoughts elsewhere. Many of us grew up with the instruction, "When you are angry, count to ten." My mother added, "If still upset, take a deep breath, begin again, and then continue the cycle until the anger subsides."

Counselors will recommend imagining the other person's point of view, coping with anger through compassion and understanding. Some of these strategies are:

- Talk through your feelings and try to work on changing your behaviors.
- Think before you act. Take time to stop and cool down when you feel yourself becoming angry.
- Identify the emotion leading you to anger such as sadness, confusion, or helplessness. Once you identify the source of your anger, analyze ways you can minimize the impact.
- Avoid situations likely to trigger your anger. For example, if heavy traffic angers you, adjust your work schedule to avoid driving during rush hour, leave home earlier and leave work later.
- Don't wait until you "blow up." Express your anger in positive ways such as giving yourself "time-out", finding a place or routine that

effectively calms your spirit, such as going for a walk or a run.

- Find a relaxing hobby such as art or listening to music.
- Journal
- When discussing your anger, use "I" statements rather than "you" statements. Say, "I don't feel valued when my needs are not being met" instead of "You make me mad when you are so inconsiderate."
- When in a conflicted relationship, listen to what the other person has to say. Seek to understand more than to be understood.
- Seek counseling.
- Forgive and forget. Forgiving helps lower blood pressure and ease muscle tension so you can feel more relaxed.
- Take care of yourself.
- Exercise regularly.
- Eat a balanced diet. Do not skip meals.
- Try to get eight hours of sleep each night.
- Limit the use of alcohol and do not use illegal drugs.

As we examine the world's solutions to avoid negative responses to anger, we realize these steps, while often temporarily helpful, stem from the belief humanity has the inner power to control its destiny.

Jesus said, "Love those who despitefully use you." Love cannot exist when self is worshipped.

For the believer, God-like love is the key to anger management. For love covers a multitude of sins and is the cornerstone for the believer's spiritual journey.

And above all things have fervent love for one another, for "love will cover a multitude of sins." (1 Peter 4:8)

Love is commitment in action.

Paul defines love as patient and kind, not envious, boastful, proud, rude, self-seeking, easily angered or calculating. Love protects, trusts, hopes, perseveres, and never fails. This is the kind of love Christ desires for the Church. His love extended. Selfless. Unconditional.

In an earlier chapter, we discussed how God calls his salt to be like him, his example of love in action.

> He who says he is in the light, and hates his brother, is in darkness until now. He who loves his brother abides in the light, and there is no cause for stumbling in him. But he who hates his brother is in darkness and walks in darkness, and does not know where he is going, because the darkness has blinded his eyes.
> (1 John 2:9–11)

The way the believer acts toward others is a tell-tale sign of the heart's condition. If Jesus is alive in us, our actions will reflect his love.

FOR FURTHER STUDY OR GROUP DISCUSSION

1. Read Titus 3:1–3.

> Remind them to be subject to rulers and authorities, to obey, to be ready for every good work, to speak evil of no one, to be peaceable, gentle, showing all humility to all men. For we ourselves were also once foolish, disobedient, deceived, serving various lusts and pleasures, living in malice and envy, hateful and hating one another.

   - Why shouldn't we speak ill of others, especially non-believers?

   - Should believers "rant" on social media? Why or why not?

- How do we maintain "love" and a peaceable attitude in a world climate that has become increasingly self-centered?

2. Read Matthew 18:21–35.

   - How does Jesus's teaching on forgiveness compare to 1 Corinthians 13:4–7?

   Love suffers long and is kind; love does not envy; love does not parade itself, is not puffed up; does not behave rudely, does not seek its own, is not provoked, thinks no evil; does not rejoice in iniquity, but rejoices in the truth; bears all things, believes all things, hopes all things, endures all things.

   - How does an attitude of unforgiveness toward even one individual impact our ability to love others?

3. Read Ephesians 4:32.

   And be kind to one another, tenderhearted, forgiving one another, even as God in Christ forgave you.

   - Why should we forgive?

- The world sees forgiveness as weakness. Why does forgiveness show strength?

4. Read 1 John 3:18.

   My little children, let us not love in word or in tongue, but in deed and in truth.

   - What are some popular phrases people might use to convey "love" in today's culture?

   - Why is action better than words?

5. Read 1 Peter 1:22–23.

   Since you have purified your souls in obeying the truth through the Spirit in sincere love of the brethren, love one another fervently with a pure heart, having been born again, not of corruptible seed but incorruptible, through the word of God which lives and abides forever …

   - Can we truly love as Christ loved through our own efforts?

   - From where do we obtain the power to truly love?

6. Read 1 John 4:7–11.

Beloved, let us love one another, for love is of God; and everyone who loves is born of God and knows God. He who does not love does not know God, for God is love. In this the love of God was manifested toward us, that God has sent His only begotten Son into the world, that we might live through Him. In this is love, not that we loved God, but that He loved us and sent His Son to be the propitiation for our sins. Beloved, if God so loved us, we also ought to love one another.

- Can we truly love apart from knowing God? Why or why not?

- How is love made possible?

7. Read Matthew 7:12.

Therefore, whatever you want men to do to you, do also to them, for this is the Law and the Prophets.

- Why do you think this is called "The Golden Rule"?

- The world's wisdom says, "Repay evil for evil." How is God's wisdom different from the vinegar of the world?

- How does this thought life help us to be love as God loves us?

Stated as the Mission of one evangelical church:

The mission of the Missionary Ministry is to continuously seek to save sinful souls by spreading the Gospel message of salvation through faith in our Lord and Savior Jesus Christ, to strengthen families by praying for them and with them, and supporting the weak and downtrodden. We do this by feeding the hungry and bereaved, providing school supplies for needy children at a local elementary school and shelter, distributing tracts, and visiting the people who are sick, shut-in, or bereaved.

- Do you agree or disagree with the methodology of answering their mission? Why or why not?

- In today's church climate, many programs are highly regulated and follow established protocols. Can we show love by following a regimen of man-made programs? Why or why not?

Conclusion

Not that I have already attained, or am already perfected;
but I press on, that I may lay hold of that for which Christ
Jesus has also laid hold of me. Brethren, I do not count
myself to have apprehended; but one thing I do, forgetting
those things which are behind and reaching forward to
those things which are ahead, I press toward the goal
for the prize of the upward call of God in Christ Jesus.
(Philippians 3:12–14)

The world has abundant wisdom. Some can be helpful.
However, God's salt, those who are called, precious in his
sight, and predestined to be in fellowship with him, need
to weigh this wisdom according to the Gospel of Truth.

The world preaches strength, truth, love, and admirable
qualities are within every spirit. If this is true, what need
do we have of a Savior? Vinegar denies the power of God
to save and transform.

What can puny man do to repay God for all his goodness?
Absolutely nothing within our human efforts. But as salt,
God wants us to take up the cup of salvation he has given us
and call upon his name. His work of grace was to reconcile
us to him, to bring us into fellowship with him as was first
intended from the foundation of the world.

Psalm 139 reminds us of this truth: Because of God's
intimate knowledge of our being, we need to be ever before
him. As his salt, God continually calls us to him, asking us
to put aside our fears, doubts, busyness, confusion, and
lift our hearts to him so he can keep our spirits refined
and pure.

He has intimate knowledge of our desire to be obedient which is at war with our human nature.

> if My people who are called by My name will humble themselves, and pray and seek My face, and turn from their wicked ways, then I will hear from heaven, and will forgive their sin and heal their land.
> (2 Chronicles 7:14)

This familiar passage was the word of the Lord given to Solomon during the dedication of the temple. The Lord told Solomon there would be times when his people would be thirsty, wander, and disregard the Lord their God.

But there was a remedy.

First of all, God is speaking to his salt—to his people. Notice the progression of return to the Lord's presence. First _____ ourselves, _____, seek his _____, and _____ from our wicked ways. _____ will I _____ and will _____your sins and _____ your land.

God's recipe for a victorious Christian life is not only possible but is God's plan for those who are called by his name.

About the Author

A veteran social worker, Linda Wood Rondeau's varied church experience and professional career affords a unique perspective into the Christian life. When not writing or speaking, she enjoys the occasional round of golf, visiting museums, and taking walks with her best friend in life, her husband of over forty years. The couple resides in Hagerstown, Maryland where both are active in their local church. Readers may learn more about the author, read her blog, or sign up for her newsletter by visiting www.lindarondeau.com.

Linda's Other Books

The Fifteenth Article

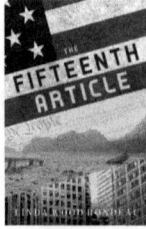

I Prayed for Patience: God Gave Me Children

Fiddler's Fling

Hosea's Heart

A Christmas Prayer

It Really IS a Wonderful Life

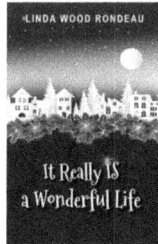

Miracle on Maple Street

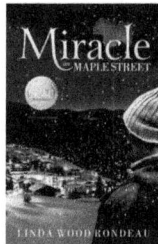

Snow on Bald Mountain